Bag the Elephant!

Bag the Elephant!

HOW TO WIN & KEEP *BIG* CUSTOMERS

BY STEVE KAPLAN

Workman Publishing, New York

Library of Congress Cataloging-in-Publication Data is available.

ISBN-13: 978-0-7611-4524-0

Workman books are available at special discounts when purchased in bulk for premiums and sales promotions as well as for fund-raising or educational use. Special editions or book excerpts also can be created to specification. For details, contact the Special Sales Director at the address below.

Design by Paul Gamarello
Photography by Steve Grubman

Author Steve Kaplan may be contacted at 312-893-5890
skaplan@stevekaplanlive.com
www.stevekaplanlive.com

Workman Publishing Company, Inc.
225 Varick Street
New York, NY 10014-4381
www.workman.com

Printed in U.S.A.
First printing January 2008

10 9 8 7 6 5 4 3 2 1

Dedication

To Andi, for your support, understanding, and patience
in putting up with the years of travel and eighteen-hour workdays
while I pursued my dreams.

To the next generation of business moguls:

Ryan, to whom everything comes so easy:
I can't wait to see the impact you're going to make on the world.

Madison, my little entrepreneur,
who at twelve has already had several successful businesses
and no doubt will rule the world someday.

To all my parents, especially my mom, Ila,
for their love and support.

To Brendi and Nanci—
from getting into trouble as little kids to having families of our own,
throughout the years you're still the best sisters and friends
I could ever ask for.

To Jules, who always has the right advice
and owns the brightest business mind I know.

Contents

Foreword

by John E. Pepper

Chairman & CEO (retired), Procter & Gamble

I found *Bag the Elephant! How to Win & Keep BIG Customers* to be a very practical and accessible presentation of how to successfully develop a long-term relationship with big clients. This book will help prepare you—and those on your team—for long-term success. It tells you how to understand the culture and the organizational structure as well as other things you need to know about major clients. It provides ideas and techniques for developing your prospect list, making winning presentations, creating champions inside your client, and negotiating the contract. It presents a value-oriented approach for building alliances, serving the clients' needs, and dealing with crises. Not least, it helps you avoid mistakes that can derail you.

This is not one of those how-to books that tries to teach some mechanical formula or addresses issues from 40,000 feet. Rather, it addresses a range of important strategic success factors with substance and straightforward language. What makes this book especially valuable is its reliance on personal and relevant stories growing from Steve Kaplan's personal experience and their presentation in a highly conversational style.

Procter & Gamble benefited significantly from Steve's experience, his ideas, and his creativity. He and his company (SCA) provided services to a large number of our brands operating across several of our divisions. During the seven years that Steve worked with P&G, he contributed insights into both our processes and our programs. He contributed to productive change within our market research, marketing operations, production, and purchasing areas. He also supported several new product introductions with his ideas and techniques.

If you gain close to the benefits that we at P&G did from the experiences and concepts which Steve communicates in his new book, you will find this a very worthwhile read.

John E. Pepper joined Procter & Gamble in 1963. He was elected group vice president in 1980, joined the board of directors in 1984, was named president of P&G in 1986, then served as CEO and chairman (1995–1999) and as chairman of the board (2000–2002). He has served on the boards of Xerox, Motorola, Boston Scientific Corporation, the Partnership for a Drug-Free America, and the National Campaign to Prevent Teen Pregnancy, as co-chair of the National Underground Railroad Freedom Center, and as chairman of the United States Advisory Committee for Trade and Policy Negotiations. He is now vice president for finance and administration of Yale University.

Preface

A Word from Steve Kaplan

Have you ever dreamed of landing that big account? That monster contract that would put you over the top? You've probably entertained the hope of dramatically increasing the size of your profits—and your paycheck. Perhaps you've already had a taste of the prosperity that can be yours when you ink the paperwork linking you with that big customer—the "Elephant."

Would you like to learn a strategy that can skyrocket your odds of winning that big payoff, hanging onto that Elephant, and repeating the accomplishment again and again?

If you're the owner of a small or medium-sized business with sales of up to $200 million, I'll tell you the ins and outs of these giant companies—what you need to know and how you need to think in order to win them over as customers. I'll show you why you don't need to be afraid of Elephants—because they need you as much as you need them. I'll give you real-world advice on how to execute a successful Bag the Elephant strategy:

- How to position your company for that huge customer
- How to select the best Elephant for you
- How to avoid the killer mistakes that can bury your company

- How to negotiate with a huge company
- How to use your Elephant as a resource for more than just profit
- How to deal with big-company demands and maximize your profits at the same time
- How to use their bureaucracy to increase your profits
- How to get all of your employees onboard a total company effort to Bag the Elephant

If you're a salesperson or sales manager, I don't have to tell you the advantages of landing those big accounts–that's something you dream about every night. I'll give you the insider information that will put you way ahead of your competitors:

- How to navigate your way through huge companies
- How to identify and secure internal champions
- How to build strong alliances within the big company to keep them needing you
- How to understand and leverage the Elephant's buying and decision-making process
- How to match the right salesperson with the right company
- How to position your sales approach for maximum effectiveness

If you're an executive or a manager in a larger company, you know how hard it is to achieve strong growth by chasing small accounts. As the person in charge of growing your department, division, or piece of the business, you'll quickly appreciate the value of an Elephant strategy. I'll show you

- How the Elephant strategy can help you to exceed your company objectives
- How to maximize profits through the Elephant process

- How to set that divisional Elephant culture
- How to set up your own bureaucracy to make the Elephant feel at home
- How to manage client expectations and respond effectively to crises
- How to recruit and cultivate champions inside the client company

If you're an accountant, artist, attorney, chiropractor, consultant, landscaper, or other professional with your own practice, you're in charge of getting clients and bringing in revenue. You probably don't spend much time thinking about getting that big new client; you may even have a distaste for selling or marketing. But when you read this book and learn about the strategy, I think you will find that it can work for you, too. I'll show you

- How to evolve to that next-level client and grow your business
- How to increase your client base using a simple, logical, proven strategy
- How to position your business to be desirable to big clients
- How to talk the language of the big company
- How to knock on prospects' doors
- How to get the most from your sales and marketing effort
- How to find the leverage you need for negotiating with your prospect

I've used this approach successfully, over and over again, to secure high-dollar business from the biggest of the big customers.

My First Elephant

Why do I think it will work for you? Because I've used this approach successfully, over and over again, to secure high-dollar business from the biggest of the big customers. I've taught it to many other business owners, salespeople, and professionals with spectacular results. It's a mindset, an attitude toward competition, a set of techniques that I put together the hard way—by personal experience over many years.

I've owned, managed, or consulted with more than 100 businesses—from runaway winners to outright dogs. One thing the winners have in common is that they all remember the exact moment they knew they had made it big. In nearly every case, that moment came when they "bagged their first Elephant"—won their first customer big enough to provide the cash flow and profits they had long craved. Then, refreshed and replenished, they could finally realize their dreams, finesse their products and services, hire more people, and capture even bigger Elephants.

Why do I call these giant companies "Elephants"? Because they are huge, slow-moving, ponderous, strong, slow to react, often loveable, sometimes stubborn—and because they require enormous amounts of input, which, if you can make it your job to supply, can bring you great financial rewards. Elephants are also smart, sometimes dangerous, uniquely individual, and equipped with long memories—all reasons for you to be super-cautious and respectful when dealing with them.

I remember exactly where I was when I got the call from my own first Elephant. It was the second year of my business. Swamped with debt, my company had been struggling to survive. My six employees and I were barely getting by, living paycheck to paycheck on meager orders from small

The Start of Something Big

Since bagging my first Elephant, I've sold to more than 100 others, including, to name just a few:

- AOL
- Citibank
- Columbia House
- Ford Motor Company
- General Foods
- General Mills
- Gruner & Jahr
- Hershey Chocolate Company
- Johnson & Johnson
- Kellogg Company
- Merck
- Nestlé Foods
- SC Johnson & Sons
- Sprint
- Time Warner
- Unilever
- a Lambert

companies. My confidence was as shaky as my bank account. Then an assistant brand manager at Procter & Gamble made the call that changed my life: he said the company had decided to give me a shot at marketing one of its products.

I had long sensed that to realize my dreams, I'd need a big company as a customer. Knowing where I needed to go was easy; the hard part was figuring out how to get there. Not only did I have no idea how big companies operated, I had no big-company contacts, minimal sales, and hardly any cash to work with. I couldn't imagine why a big company would have any interest in a small company like mine.

I decided to target Procter & Gamble, but I knew it would be an uphill fight. For starters, I lived in Chicago, but Procter & Gamble operated out of Cincinnati. Because my company was running on fumes, I had to slash costs however I could. I borrowed a friend's car to chauffeur my clients around when they came to town—my own car was a beater that stalled about 50 percent of the time. I parked at airport hotels so I could slip inside their free airport shuttle buses. And because I had only one suit, I had to schedule meetings so I wouldn't run into the same people twice.

Unless you've actually built and operated a successful business yourself, you can't really understand the true concerns of the business owner.

Fast-forward five years, and my once-tiny company was being paid close to $30 million a year by P&G to help it market more than fifty products, including such well-known brands as Tide, Crest, Scope, and Pringles.

Over the years, I nurtured these early relationships with P&G and other large corporate customers until some of my colleagues and I were sitting in on many high-level strategy sessions with them as they decided how to launch their newest products—a display of confidence that most suppliers in our industry could only dream of.

It didn't happen by accident. The strategy that got me there paved the way for more gratifying relationships with other large corporations. In the end, my company grew into the largest business in its industry. I set out to grow my business by selling to Elephants, and I achieved so much success with this strategy that I eventually became an Elephant myself, with annual sales of $250 million.

The Missing Ingredient

Over the past ten years, I've delved into the inner workings of large corporate bureaucracies and have been able to capitalize on these insights to help small companies grab a share of their business.

But when I was starting out, I scrambled around for advice, data, or anything else that might help me snag a big customer. What I needed in my life was someone with practical knowledge, experience, and a record of success who was willing to spend the time to make the difference in my business. The problem for me—and, I imagine, for you—is that no one like this existed. Friends and family can't help; unless you've actually built and operated a successful business yourself, you can't really understand the true concerns of the business owner. You won't know what it's like to sacrifice time away from family and friends, lying awake at 3:00 AM beating yourself up over a mistake you may have made, or feeling the pressure of worrying about not only providing for your loved ones but protecting your employees and their families.

This is why I wrote *Bag the Elephant!,* the first in a series of books designed to provide a firsthand approach to solving the real issues of business owners, managers, salespeople, and professionals. This book addresses head-on many of the doubts that are probably going through your mind right now:

- "My business doesn't lend itself to big customers."

One of the first things this book will show you is that almost any business in any industry can get big customers—it's just a matter of knowing where to look.

- "I wouldn't even know where to begin."

Beginning is the toughest part. Once you've made the commitment, it gets easier.

- "I've tried to get big customers, but it just didn't work out."

Chances are at the time you didn't know what you needed to succeed. You may have gone after the wrong customer or mischaracterized your pitch. Try again, using my Bag the Elephant strategy.

Your Secret Weapon

Imagine that you know how big companies operate, know how to position yourself and your business to meet big customers' needs, know what roadblocks may impede success, know which pitfalls to avoid, and know how best to approach, negotiate, and bag your Elephants. I'd hate to be your competitor!

I have personal experience that affirms how important this knowledge is for everyone in your business. I've been a sales rep, a team member, and a business owner.

When I was growing my first business, I sold in the daytime and ran the business at night. Even when my company was at the $15 million level, I still accounted for 90 percent of its sales.

Much of what I've learned, the knowledge I wish to pass along to you, came out of my view from the other end of the telescope. I know how Elephants think, what Elephants feel, how Elephants act, because not only have I sought after and sold to Elephants, I've been the Elephant that other business owners, professional practitioners, and salespeople have sought to corral. I know what the big guys look for when they're buying.

Bag the Elephant! is the distillation of that knowledge. Now that you've got it, here's how to use it.

Read the book—the whole book—and be sure you understand the complete strategy. Don't just dip in here and there or skip chapters looking for clever tactics to use. It's the whole package that works; the overall strategy is far more important than the individual procedures or tactics. It's also important to absorb the nuances, the many details that make the difference between a thorough understanding and a superficial acquaintance with the strategy. Be sure to visit my Web site, www.differencemaker.com, as well. I set up this Web site to give you access to more tools—charts, templates, and worksheets—to guide you in your quest. You can download many of these tools at no cost.

Share it with your sales force. This book represents a decade of experience in capturing large customers. All material is my work, and it's been used many times with much success. The concepts and strategies should be communicated to your sales staff. After all, they're directly involved in the effort, and the approach I discuss will help them increase overall sales.

Share it with your whole team. Whether you have one employee or a thousand, you'll need to instill the "big customer" culture throughout your business. It's a group effort, and the material in this book will go far in getting everyone on the same page.

This isn't a feel-good book; I'm not just going to tell you what I think you want to hear. It's not a "business-speak" book; you won't find me using trendy business clichés like "win-win," "synergy," or "holistic." What you'll find is straight talk about growing your business by getting big customers and keeping them loyal to you.

I had to learn the secrets in this book the hard way—by trial and error, accident and determination, mistakes and triumphs over many years. You, however, sitting in an armchair or on a plane or train for a few hours, can learn the basics well enough to take them into the field and start seriously pursuing those giant contracts.

Getting that big customer requires a big commitment. If you're willing to take responsibility for the success or failure of your business, and if you're ready to make the commitment necessary to change, this is the book for you. Read it, use it, and watch your business succeed beyond your wildest expectations. Stay the course, and that success can change your life.

The Elephants are waiting.

—Steve Kaplan

Part I
YOUR ELEPHANT
IS WAITING

The Third Path

Achieving Lasting Growth and Profits

There are three basic business stories. No matter whether it's a giant multinational corporation or a mom-and-pop corner store, based in a home office or a giant office complex, every business that gets off the ground follows one of three basic paths. It's a simple fact of life in the business world. What makes this fact somewhat scary is that only one of these paths leads to lasting prosperity.

This third path, the one that brings you out on top, is not an easy or foolproof path. It is strewn with obstacles and dangers; it takes brains, guts, and a lot of hard work. To get on this path and follow it to success, you have to do one of two things: either make a lot of small sales to more and more small buyers, or make a few big sales to a few big customers.

In my experience, it's better to sell to a few big customers. Why? Because you can do it quicker, with fewer staff, with less capital investment, less advertising—and it's easier to develop meaningful relationships.

So—why don't you find most business, sales, and professional people on my road to big-company sales success? Two big reasons:

- Many business owners, executives, sales professionals, and private practitioners would rather have a very large number of customers because they feel it's safer, and because they like the idea of running a large company with massive capital investment and hundreds or thousands of employees.

- Many of the rest—those who see the advantages of the big-customer strategy—either don't know how to go about it or are afraid to take what they see as a path strewn with risks.

This means the big-company path, the road to rapid, sustainable growth through the cultivation of a few big customers, is open to you—if you understand the principles, strategies, and tactics and execute them better than your competitors.

First, though, let's look at the three pathways, so you can see more clearly what you've got to avoid, as well as the one true path that will bring you out in the right place.

The Trail of the Snail

Don Clark owns Dive Right In, a neighborhood store in Phoenix specializing in above-ground pools, pool supplies, and outdoor gas grills. Although he's been in business six years and puts in sixty hours a week, he's barely staying afloat. He ekes out about 3 percent growth a year, just ahead of inflation. (Three percent growth might be fine if you're a big company, but Dive Right In is not.) No matter how Don has tried to breathe life into his company—varying his product line, hiring more salespeople—he never sees the results he needs. Instead, he's resigned to waiting for a miracle to fall from the sky. He's in a rut.

Don's story is all too common. In fact, more than half the business owners I evaluate are on the Snail Trail. Their lives

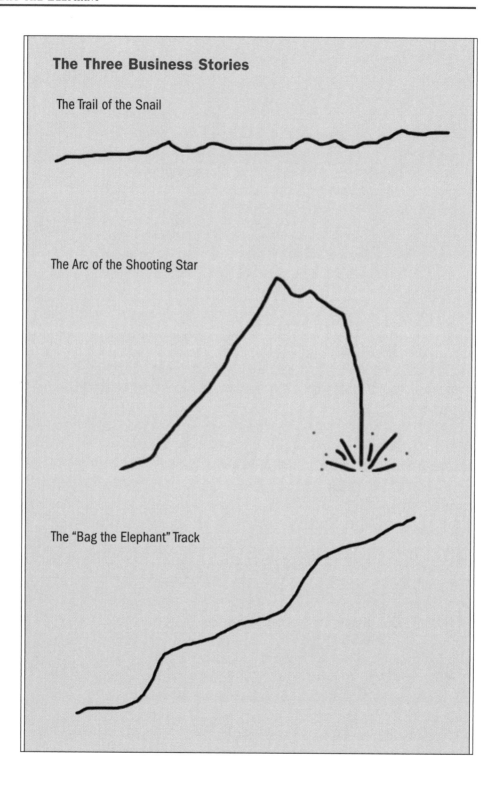

The Three Business Stories

The Trail of the Snail

The Arc of the Shooting Star

The "Bag the Elephant" Track

are their livelihoods; they grind away at it, but they never reap the rewards.

Why does this happen?

Don, like so many others, has became a victim of his own devotion. He gives his all to making his store a success and fools himself into thinking success is just around the corner. His identity is wrapped up in his business. In fact, this emotional investment has so clouded his judgment that even his life savings are at risk. He can no longer face hard facts.

In most cases, lackluster businesses stay that way because the owner sees no way out.

Other business people end up on the Snail Trail simply because of financial strain. They've got three kids in school, a mortgage, two car payments, four maxed-out credit cards, and no margin for error. They know something has to change, but they're afraid to rock the boat (also bought on credit). What if they lose the trickle of income that keeps them afloat?

The fear of change can span generations in a business, getting stronger all the time. A father brings his sons and daughters into the business, hoping an infusion of youth will bring growth. But when they suggest improvements that entail necessary risks, he resists, and the lethargic business stays stuck in its rut, having to support more and more households.

In most cases, lackluster businesses stay that way because the owner sees no way out. In particular, the owner cannot figure out how to snag the one big client that could be the answer to the company's prayers.

Businesses that continue down the Snail Trail are living on the edge. They have little resilience. Any glitch could be their downfall. Events beyond their control—illness, economic downturn, an increase in the price of raw materials, the loss of a key employee, a delay in receivables—could also prove fatal.

If you follow the Trail of the Snail, you'll probably run out of time before you run out of road.

The Arc of the Shooting Star

Rob and Jeff are great friends. They attended college together and cooperated on some odd jobs, then became business partners. Rob is a sales genius, Jeff an operations wiz.

Both men are electronic buffs. Working out of Rob's home, they buy old electronics appliances from flea markets and garage sales for about ten cents on the dollar. Inside Rob's garage, using such high-tech tools as toothbrushes and soldering guns, they clean the rust and dust off the old parts, disassemble and refurbish them, and sell them to local manufacturers and hardware stores. Their labor costs are minimal—mostly their own time, supplemented by free labor from friends who take pity on them. Their cutthroat pricing, however, shows the competition no mercy.

This happens to a third of all businesses. Sales skyrocket, more people are hired, everyone is smiling—and suddenly it's all over.

Rob, a master relationship builder, begins snuggling up to several large companies, which start generating large profits for the two men. Then they move into a small complex and hire some real employees to help out. Rob eventually persuades a leading appliance manufacturer to sign a $12 million parts contract.

The deal begets many others. Before Rob and Jeff can catch their breath, the twenty-seven-year-old college buddies are raking in sales of almost $200 million per year. They've hired more than 150 employees, automated their refurbishing process, and bought a swanky complex with a swimming pool and racquetball court. They've blazed above the business horizon like a shooting star. They can't believe their luck.

Thirteen months later, their star fizzles and falls from the sky.

This happens to at least a third of the businesses I've observed. At first, they grow fast. Sales skyrocket, more people are hired, everyone is smiling—and then, suddenly, it's all over.

What's happening here?

More likely than not, this business has fallen victim to its own success. In more than 90 percent of Shooting Star companies I've seen, the business reaches a new level of success by generating lots of business from big customers. The usual small-business problems that once nagged—meeting payroll, short-term cash flow—become distant memories, not worth thinking about. Now, rather than worrying about how to make ends meet, the owners worry about what they'll do with all their money. It's euphoria time.

While it lasts, that is. In most cases, one of the following stumbling blocks emerges:

- The business attracts more and more customers but lets its operations lag.
- With success comes greater customer service expectations—standards that the business cannot yet meet.
- New customer demands leave no time for long-term planning and strategy; the owners barely have time to satisfy short-term customer needs.

The result? The big clients that once generated so much excitement become disenchanted and eventually withdraw. But because of the "burn rate" from paying for all the new hires and expansion, coupled with the reduction in cash flow, the business meets a sudden and ugly crash.

In short, the Shooting Star business falls out of the sky because it fails to perform two tasks that are key to its survival:

- Capture more big customers to feed its growing business
- Ratchet up the business's infrastructure to meet those big customers' needs and demands.

After a year or so of healing, Rob and Jeff get back on the horse. Jeff goes to work for a large electronics company in the Chicago area. Rob opens another business, an online company specializing in finding and reselling liquidated items. Using his big-customer experience, he's been able to align with yet another big client, but this time he's being much smarter about managing his growth.

The "Bag the Elephant" Track

In Austin, Texas, far from the big-city advertising centers of New York and Chicago, six new University of Texas graduates decide in 1971 to form their own ad agency, GSD&M, with a bold new vision: using big ideas to get big results, to "create something that was not there before." From the beginning, they seek to ally themselves with big companies.

One of those big companies is Southwest Airlines, headed by Herb Kelleher, its irreverent and charismatic chairman/CEO/president. By 1981, after only ten years, Southwest is already a major player, with over a quarter of a billion dollars in annual revenue—and growing fast.

Sensing a rare opportunity to hitch their wagon to a rising star, GSD&M, led by founder Roy Spence, pitches an innovative ad campaign based on the idea of "flying for peanuts." Southwest buys it and becomes the agency's first Elephant in 1981. In the years that follow, GSD&M and Southwest grow and prosper together. Southwest turns again and again to the ambitious, visionary ad agency that helped it achieve its early marketing success—and they're still together, with GSD&M creating the lion's share of Southwest's advertising.

With the kick-start provided by this first big client, GSD&M becomes the third-largest advertising agency in the United States ($1.5 billion annual revenue) by signing other big clients, such as Sam Walton's revolutionary Wal-Mart, as well as DreamWorks, PGA Tour, MasterCard, AARP, Charles Schwab, and the U.S. Olympic Committee. GSD&M's new "Idea City"—in reality, its Austin headquarters—is a wildly creative environment with separate "neighborhoods" for copywriters and financial planners, thirty "war rooms" designed to foster creative thinking, a Ping-Pong table in a soundproofed room, even a life-size stuffed cow on a pulley. Known for its innovative work, GSD&M, now a

You Can Win Big if You Do Four Things

• Attract, keep, and leverage big clients.

• Acquire the strategic and tactical expertise you need to scale up your business.

• Instill a big-business culture.

• Have the courage to make the changes needed to grow.

subsidiary of the Omnicon Group, has been named "Agency of the Year" six times by *AdWeek* magazine.

Obviously GSD&M's winning path—following the "Bag the Elephant" Track—is where you want to be. That's the easy part, as you know. But getting there is much harder—so much harder that very few businesses ever find their way.

To be one of these happy few, get to know how GSD&M differed from its cohorts on the Shooting Star path, who were consumed with skyrocketing growth at all costs. Unlike them, companies like GSD&M usually grow steadily, even vigorously, but always under control, never letting their customer list outpace their infrastructure.

Sure, it's a long road, but it's worth the trip, because

- Continued success, growth, and profits will let you reap the financial gains a successful business can bring in.
- Selling the business to another company will allow you to capture your company's earnings or revenues many times over—as well as a chance to make a graceful exit.
- Merging with another company will typically yield you some cash and let you align with another company that facilitates faster growth.
- Family succession will let you spend time with your loved ones and help them succeed, all while earning money.

Although almost all business, sales, and professional people fancy themselves on this winning path, the truth is that most of them are actually on the Trail of the Snail or the Arc of the Shooting Star. This is not necessarily a death sentence, of course. Many on the Snail Trail are able to pay their bills well enough to get by, and some Shooting Stars manage to relight themselves and blaze anew across the sky.

But neither of these paths promises you a good chance of surviving and thriving over the long haul. You're more likely to end up among the tens of thousands of businesses in the U.S. that quietly fizzle or spectacularly flame out every year.

If you're on one of the first two paths, realizing as much is the first step. And if you're just getting started, now's the time to make sure you're headed down the third path—the one that leads to lasting success and prosperity.

You've Got
to Believe

Elephants Need You, Too

Emily and Meghan, sisters and avid photographers, run a custom-stationery business out of their homes. They call it Touching Memories. The women convert photographs into personalized note pads, letterhead, or anything else their customers wish. The quality is high and the pricing low. Their biggest problem, by far, has been driving sales.

I got together with Emily and Meghan two years ago to seek solutions. Sure, they needed more customers, but who? At the time, 100 percent of their customers were individuals, mostly moms who wanted stationery featuring their children.

We spoke at length about how to expand their customer base to include larger clients who could buy in bigger quantities. One idea was to approach a major retail store that could carry their product line and promote it to the hundreds of thousands of shoppers who traipsed through the mall every year. Another was to seek out large companies that might want to buy the custom stationery as unique gifts for their employees or clients. After weighing both plans, the sisters bet the farm on corporate gifts.

First they selected a handful of large companies to pursue. They pored over lists from *Fortune* magazine's "Best Companies to Work for in America," as well as other sources, and sought out champions at the ones located near their city. They worked to establish solid relationships at these companies. Eventually this approach yielded deals with three large companies that wound up placing more than 100 orders their first year.

Later, we met again to see if we could do even better. The sisters said they would like to work toward opening a small store while extracting a higher volume of business from their big customers.

Not long ago, they sent me an e-mail brimming with excitement. In just a few months' time they had filled more than 1,000 orders, and they were expecting another 2,000 by year's end—all from their original three big customers. They were doing so well that, rather than opening a store, they decided to stick with their easier, less expensive—and enormously profitable—Elephant strategy.

Emily and Meghan are living proof of how motivated entrepreneurs, no matter how small their operations, can break down the doors of large companies and walk away with enough business to keep them busy for years.

A Daunting Prospect

Not that it's always so easy. In my own career, when I first realized I needed large companies as clients, the task seemed an impossible dream. But that was because I didn't understand how big companies operated and hadn't a clue how to get in the door. On the other hand, I knew my own business, and I was confident that, if given the chance, I'd be able to deliver.

When I set my sights on Procter & Gamble, I was aware, of course, that I faced long odds. Still, only a few years later, not only was my company a preferred P&G vendor, our growing credibility with other large corporate clients found us sitting in on their high-level new-product brainstorming sessions as well.

If you think there's a catch, you're right—and it's a real Catch-22. As an overcommitted, overscheduled salesperson,

Baby Elephant to the Rescue

Anne Morgan was a real estate agent working at a typical huge real estate company. She sold homes in the Westchester area of New York and, as is the case with most real estate agents, earned all her income from commissions. Anne was doing pretty well but was hungry for more, and a bit frustrated. Her life sometimes seemed to be a never-ending search for that next house to sell.

One day Anne was showing a house to an executive who was moving there to take a new job. Earlier that week, Anne had met another person in the same situation. Then it hit her. She knew how she could break away from her day-to-day struggle: by bagging an Elephant.

In her case, the Elephant would be a huge business that relocated executives. What a great thing, she thought, if she could manage to be the person these big companies turned to when they needed to move someone into her area.

Diligently and tenaciously, she went after huge multinational corporations by pitching to the human resources and benefits people. She did so for over a year— and one day she got her chance. The real estate firm one of these companies was using had dropped the ball; it was hers to run with. She did a great job for her Elephant and eventually became the authorized agent in her area for one division of a multinational Elephant. In the very first year alone, this baby Elephant helped her more than double her already high commission income.

business owner, or professional, where do you find the time to go looking for that big customer? Whether you're caught up in the hurly-burly of delivering to your existing clients or frantically scrambling to drum up a customer or two, how can you possibly find the time to devote a part of every workweek to bagging that big client?

But that's what you have to do in order to achieve that quantum leap in growth and income that you're after. You have to treat your Elephant hunting as a vital activity at the core of your daily or weekly routine, no matter what other fires are blazing. Landing that big client isn't a luxury or a spare-time function; it's the key to big profits.

When it comes to getting business from large companies, you can't just pick a name out of the phonebook and knock on doors until someone lets you in. It's not that simple. Still, virtually every huge corporation needs smaller businesses as suppliers. In each case, someone has to get the account—and it might as well be you.

Getting these prime clients doesn't mean being a slick, fast-talking corporate cowboy. It does mean presenting yourself as someone who listens to clients and meets their needs.

First, you have to know a lot about how big companies operate, particularly how they decide to buy a product or service. Then you have to figure out which of your prospective clients are best for you. Only then can you map out a strategy for approaching them, not just by putting your wares in the best possible light but also by seeking someone at the company to champion you and your business.

To show how this works, I'll use a variety of examples, many from my experiences with Procter & Gamble, others from my success with another 100 or so Elephants. (I've changed the names to protect the proprietary information and privacy of my clients.) The same strategies have been used for all types and sizes of businesses in a wide variety of industries. When you read the examples, think about how they relate to your business. They won't be point-to-point the same, but there are many ways you can apply the lessons to your situation.

On the next page is a table showing the success achieved by some of the companies I've worked with, including my own, SCA. Although I can't promise that you'll bag a mega-corporation like P&G, I will say that nearly any business can land at least one large company as a client and, by doing so, greatly increase its chances for big-time success.

The Elephants Need You

Perhaps the first barrier to overcome is the belief that large companies have no use for your goods or services.

Paula Westman owned a small CPA firm that specialized in tax returns. She had a pretty nice practice preparing about 250 tax returns per year for individuals and smaller businesses, billing just over $300,000 annually. It had taken Paula about fifteen years to get to this point, and she was clearly getting burned out. She lived with the pressures of being a one-woman band, including the concern that her business would collapse should she happen to become ill during peak

Businesses That Have Grown by Bagging a Few Elephants

Company	Industry	Growth*	Positioning	Elephants
SCA	Marketing, promotion	From $200,000 to $30,000,000	Product expansion database, targeted marketing	Packaged-goods companies
Jot It Down	Quick print	From $120,000 to $2,000,000	Deadline printing with big-company pickup	Local large firms in several industries
CPA Marketplace	Tax returns	From $220,000 to $780,000	Executive tax returns at volume discount (company perk)	Fortune 500 company
Touching Memories	Custom stationery	From $50,000 to $500,000	Gifts for employees & clients	Fortune 500 company
AEO Plumbing	Plumbing	From $80,000 to $600,000	Emergency service for developer, plumbing for development	Large residential developer
Apex Realty	Real estate	From $1,000,000 to $8,000,000	Housing for relocated executives	Two large Fortune 500 companies
Happy Dog Walking	Dog walking	From $8,000 to $52,000	Dog walking for executives	Large computer company
TradingPost.com	Online collectibles	From $20,000 to $2,000,000	eBay feeder alliance	eBay
Snyder Communications	Advertising	From $100,000 to $50,000,000+	Product expansion telemarketing	AT&T
Simply Sweet	Retail store confection	From $70,000 to $1,000,000	Distribution	Large catalog & high-end chain
SpeedByte	At-home PC consulting	From $15,000 to $400,000	Outsource capability for large companies	Several huge companies
Specialty Finance	High-risk lending	From $500,000 to $6,000,000	Higher-risk loans Higher interest rates	Underwriting banks
Smith-Ballenberg	Printing broker	From $2,000,000 to $14,000,000	A.S.A.P. NOW service	Packaged goods company
JPS Appraising	Appraisal service	From $50,000 to $2,000,000	Dedicated appraisal staff & service	Large lender banks

*annual sales

tax season. She desperately wanted to expand her business so that she could hire other CPAs to help carry the load.

Clearly Paula needed to bag an Elephant, but being in the service industry posed some unique challenges. Not the least of these was the fact that she couldn't imagine large companies needing her services. I sat down with her to figure out the best strategy for the hunt.

We decided to focus on large corporations, like Viacom, Motorola, and Kraft, that provided tax planning benefits to their middle and senior management. After much industry research, we found that large companies did provide executives perks. We further learned that tax planning and financial services offered to the executives were provided through a few select businesses. The challenge then became how to become one of these lucky three or four firms that would provide a guaranteed 200-plus returns a year.

Paula went at it. She had much to do: selecting the right prospect company, determining needs, positioning her firm to meet those needs, identifying champions within the company, process building, and much more. A solid year of hard work paid off, and Paula got her first company client. She worked out a deal with her Elephant that guaranteed her 225 returns per year for the next five years. This allowed her to hire three full-time junior CPAs to assist. Since then, Paula's firm has landed three more corporate clients, and she now handles 1,000 returns annually. Her firm now handles only corporations, which use her firm as a benefit to their executives.

Here's a not-insubstantial side benefit: now that Paula's firm has guaranteed contracts that run well into the future, she has a wonderful business to sell at a nice premium, should she choose.

An important first step in bagging your first Elephant is to get over the assumption that no large company could possibly be interested in what you have to offer. The truth is, the Elephant needs you almost as much as you need the Elephant. And as you'll see, after you've been together awhile—after the Elephant has come to depend on your products or services, and you've become a larger, more powerful enterprise with other big clients—the Elephant may end up needing you more than you need the Elephant.

Part II
THE SECRET LIFE
OF THE ELEPHANT

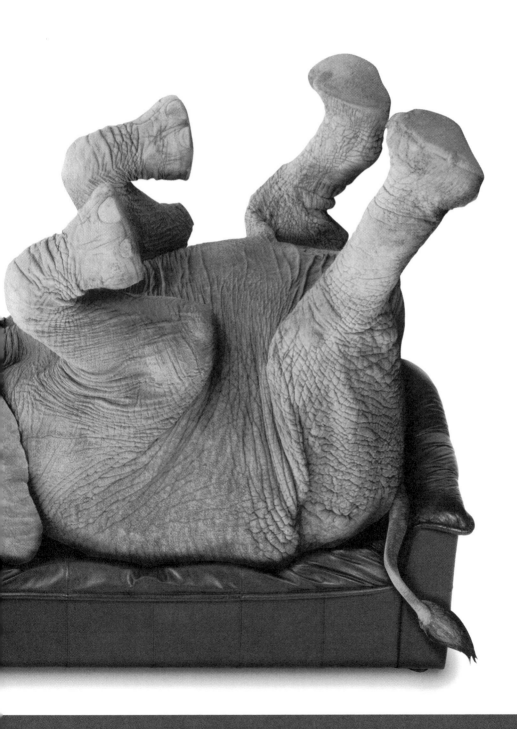

The Big-
Company Focus

Learning to Think Like an Elephant

There are many things you have to do in order to pursue, capture, and hold onto your Elephant. First among these is to get your mind right.

How's that again?

All right, I'll explain. You have to change your outlook. You have to stop thinking like a business your size and start thinking like an Elephant.

Why? Not because you expect to become an Elephant—at least not right away. You learn to think like an Elephant so you can get inside your Elephant's head. It's important that you see things from the Elephant's point of view.

Getting your mind right means not just you, as head of your business or as a crackerjack lone-wolf salesperson. It means everyone in your business—every person who will be engaged in hunting your Elephant, every executive, manager, accountant, service representative, delivery person, mechanic, creative writer, and board member your Elephant might come in contact with. It includes everyone, of course, because everyone in your business has a part and a stake in bagging your Elephant and keeping it happy.

It's a total team effort, top to bottom. You can't have salespeople fully committed and connected with the needs of the prospective big customer while the rest of your organization operates under a different set of guidelines.

To ensure your best chance for success, you must get everyone working together toward a common goal. All decisions about the customer, the way your employees or associates approach prospective customer requests, the speed, priority, and accuracy with which work gets done—all affect your chances for success.

> **Six Keys to the Elephant**
>
> • One and Done
>
> • Priority One
>
> • Whatever It Takes
>
> • Long-Term Vision
>
> • Breath of Fresh Air
>
> • Partners

Six Keys to a Big-Customer Focus

To help you focus on getting inside the mind of an Elephant, I'll describe for you my six keys to achieving the right mindset. These are attitudes and habits that you should cultivate (or, in some cases, guard against) in yourself and your business if you're serious about bagging and keeping that big, rich customer.

One and Done

You're working overtime at getting the big customer. You've been able to hold a few meetings and have had some success at building a good rapport with your Elephant. In fact, the prospect just gave you several projects to quote and asked that you get them back ASAP. You assure him he'll have the quotes within a couple of days. You submit the details, along with a rush notice to your company for the quotes. You're actually beginning to think that the past six months of work on this account just might pay off.

Three days go by, and no quote. You check with your operations people; they tell you they're having trouble pricing out one of the components. You reiterate the importance of these quotes. Another two days go by, and the prospect actually calls you for the first time. But it isn't to place an order or to thank you for a job well done; instead, it's to ask, with obvious impatience, "Where's that quote you promised me?"

> **You're going to be working very hard for one shot at a potential client— and if you blow it, you're done.**

The "one and done" principle is simple. You're going to be working very hard with the hope of getting one shot at a potential client—and if you blow it, you're done. This means everything from the initial contact forward, including quotes, presentations, sales pitches, client requests, and—even after you've signed a deal—delivery and further sales. Though your business may be the best thing around, the big company may never find out if it doesn't hire you. Don't give your prospect any reason to doubt you or look elsewhere, not even for a moment.

Priority One

Everyone wants to feel special. Big customers are no different. Depending on your industry, many suppliers offer similar products and services. Sometimes the supplier that gets the business is the one that gives the best service or offers a uniquely valuable "extra."

It's a tricky balancing act. On the one hand, you want the client to feel she's your only customer—while at the same time giving her the impression you have lots of other satisfied customers in your stable. Even though the big company wants to feel that it's being given special treatment and attention, it also likes to have its judgment in doing business with you validated by other big companies.

Lavish plenty of attention on your Elephant. Make that big company feel looked after and cherished. Return calls speedily. Answer questions quickly. Address problems immediately. Be kind to your Elephant, and it will be kind to you.

Whatever It Takes

If you've done a good job of looking after your client, your reputation for top-flight work will have spread throughout the company, where new opportunities await. Some of these opportunities may seem removed from your core business.

This is no time to grow fainthearted. Think flexible; consider bending over backward and touching your head to the floor if necessary. Even if your current product line keeps you hopping, be grateful for the chance to grow. If you can, adjust your business plans on the fly to adapt.

When a corporate client asked Touching Memories, the custom stationery suppliers, to include calendars, this was something the sisters had never done. They were up to their ears in notepad and letterhead jobs. Still, they thought, why not? Best of all, the corporation agreed to fund the startup costs by placing a large order up front. This enabled Touching Memories to develop the new product at a profit. Calendars are now their biggest sellers—thanks to flexibility.

Flexibility comes in many forms. It might be as simple as invoicing early or late so that a client can use monies from a desired budget or time frame, setting meeting times to suit their schedule, pushing a delivery date up or back, or inventorying specified items.

It also might mean the opportunity to expand your services. Throughout my years of running a targeted-marketing business and working with Procter & Gamble and other big companies, I made it a point to position my company as innovative and "can do." I never put limits on what could or couldn't be done. If the price was right and we could maintain our customary quality and service, we would always do the job, whatever it was. I worked to convey this approach throughout my company and was shocked to see just how many immediately profitable new business ideas came to us simply because we were flexible.

Long-Term Vision

Pigs get fat; hogs get slaughtered. Sure, you can expect to make a lot of money doing business with your Elephant, but don't get greedy. You must be careful to view your big customer as a partner in a long-term relationship. Once you've established this relationship of mutual trust, there will be plenty of revenue available to you. However, many are those who try to break the bank on their first big score and end up paying the price. An Elephant that feels it is being gouged can depart in a hurry—and do a lot of damage on the way out. Believe me, these large clients understand how much they mean to a smaller business like yours, and they remain vigilant.

> **Don't get greedy. View your big customer as a partner in a long-term relationship.**

Think of your big customers as stepping-stones for success. If you want to get to the top, you might need several stones, and each one should be as high as possible—but not out of reach of the one before. Go slow and enjoy the ride. If you get greedy, you'll price yourself right out of the opportunity. (I'm not suggesting that you lower your pricing to get the big customer; in fact, there are cases where your pricing should actually be a bit higher than usual. What I'm saying is, don't expect to buy your Montana ranch and retire after one sale.)

Breath of Fresh Air

Work should be fun. This is something I believe, big time. If you're not having fun, you should find other work. It's important for two reasons:

- Having fun is good for business. People work better when they're having fun. Look at Southwest Airlines, Seattle's Pike Place Fish Market, BNI (Business Network International), and other thriving businesses that emphasize fun.

- Potential clients should feel that working with your business will be a pleasant experience. It strengthens the relationship.

Having fun—and showing it—is a great way to distinguish yourself from your competitors, most of whom will be so focused on getting the dollars that they'll forget about the relationship, which often is what got them the business in the first place.

Having fun—and showing it—is a way to distinguish yourself from your competitors.

If prospects or customers call your business and speak to anyone—receptionist, salesperson, customer service rep, or the guy who fills the soap dispensers—they should have a favorable experience. I never put up with anything less than a pleasant interaction between my employees and any customer.

When you call on a prospect, make sure to tell him a funny story, recount something interesting that happened that day, or take him out for lunch and talk about sports or family. I always had an anecdote ready as an icebreaker. Be friendly, but don't impose yourself on the prospect. Show respect, but don't suck up. Toot the other person's horn rather than your own. Instead of overstaying your welcome or wasting his time, make a timely exit and leave him looking forward to your next visit. The same goes for anyone else who makes the call.

I used to tell my employees the best compliment they can ever have from a big customer is to be described as professional, knowledgeable, and great to work with.

Partners

A partnership is a two-way street—and that's how you should approach your relationship with your big customer. Yes, your Elephant can do you enormous favors. Your relationship can be a fountainhead of revenues and profits for many years if you nurture it. But on the other side, you're in a position to do great favors for your Elephant, too. You may even make yourself an indispensable partner.

Seek ways to help your Elephant. Look for processes and methods for streamlining its operations. Look for ways to save it money. You have a lot to offer; your products, your services, or simply your habit of delivering reliably, promptly, and effectively may be pivotal to your Elephant's survival and prosperity. Your big-company partner may even grow to feel that its own well-being is closely tied to that of your business, giving it added incentive to treat you well.

Seek ways to help your Elephant streamline its operations and save money.

Don't give away the store in hopes of wooing a prospective big client. Approach the relationship with the goal of finding the best deal that can both (1) fill your client's needs and (2) keep your business healthy and growing. Don't underestimate what you can bring to the table. If you become a valued resource by virtue of acting quickly and effectively, your odds of success skyrocket.

Tactics

All well and good, you say. You've told us how a big-company focus looks, sounds, and smells. Now can you give me some down-to-earth advice on just how to instill the big-company focus throughout my business?

The answer is yes. Here are seven tactics that cover much of the territory:

Signage. I used to have a sign prominently posted in my company that simply listed the six keys to big-customer success. I referred my employees to it often as we embarked on our quest to bag the Elephant.

Team meetings. To be successful, you need a team approach. Everyone likes to feel part of an effort, especially when it ends up being successful. Every week, hold a short meeting to talk about big-customer progress and issues. Don't just talk about salespeople and leave out everyone else; lavish praise on everyone who helped out, whether in sales, operations, customer service, or accounting. Acknowledge those who worked on a proposal or a quote. It's a good way to treat your employees, and it will make them work twice as hard to get an honorable mention at the next meeting.

Performance-based compensation. In my company, every employee received a regular bonus, 60 percent of which was based on personal performance, 40 percent on the company's performance—which included bagging Elephants. This policy was highly effective in focusing people's attention on getting that big customer, no matter what department they were in.

A **"right now" policy.** When an Elephant calls you, it's usually because he has found a free minute or two. You never know when that brief window will open again. That's why you've got to return an Elephant's call promptly.

> **When an Elephant calls you, it's usually because he has found a free minute or two. You never know when that brief window will open again.**

At all my businesses, I've made it a policy for employees to contact me immediately whenever a prospect called, so I could return the call right away. What's more, anytime a big prospect or a current Elephant called, whoever answered the phone would try to reach the target employee through normal routing or, if the employee was on the phone or away from her desk, by getting up and tracking her down. If she was out of the office, she was called on her cell phone and asked to return the call immediately.

Does this sound a bit over the top? Well, it worked. Our average time between the first ring and talking with the prospect dropped from a few hours to a few minutes.

Awards and recognition. I found it effective to give quarterly awards for outstanding big-customer development. We'd order pizza for lunch, then award complimentary lunch certificates to a couple of high-performing employees. No big deal, on the face of it, but the recognition meant a lot to the salespeople who got them. I also gave out more prestigious awards—handsome Lucite recognition plaques—at our annual holiday dinner.

Training and certification. Whenever I hired new employees, I made sure that their training included a solid understanding of the six keys to big-customer success, including their expected role in bagging the Elephant. As part of their annual performance review, my employees were rated on their adherence to the six keys to big-customer

---

CERTIFICATE OF QUALIFICATION

Big-Customer Team_____
Customer Name

This certificate confirms that _____has
completed Big-Customer Protocol training in the following Big-
Customer criteria:

One and Done	Priority One
Whatever It Takes	Long-Term Vision
Breath of Fresh Air	Partners

_____   _____
President   Team Member

_____
Date

---

success. This had a positive effect. They embraced the keys, and everyone—employees, the company, the big customer— was better off for it.

I found it very effective to reward employees I had placed on big-customer teams by giving them what I call "credential with proof." I created a simple certificate verifying that the named employee had completed big-customer training and understood the essentials of bagging an Elephant, including the six keys.

I was amazed at how well these worked, but if you think about it, the reason is simple. The employees actually received proof that they had accomplished something in the workplace. Being named to an elite team and trained to achieve the team goals enhanced their value in the open marketplace. And, let's face it, a wise employee is constantly seeking ways to enhance her paycheck or power base.

The other reason this tactic worked so well was that it encouraged the employee and team member to take pride in her work. Being named to the team, and then actually signing the certificate with the rules spelled out, obligated her to perform at the desired level. This is just human nature, but it results in better performance for you as the team leader or employer.

> **A wise employee is constantly seeking ways to enhance her paycheck or power base.**

Looking the Part

There's another reason to cultivate a big-company focus inside your own business, sales team, or private practice: Elephants like to do business with partners who think and act like themselves. It's not that you have to be a giant to play with the giants—you just have to show them you know the rules of their game and can play by them.

Perception is one of the rules—how you are perceived by your client. You may not be a fellow Elephant, but if you can play the part, you're halfway there. When you go to meetings, dress as well as your client. This will give you confidence, and when your confidence shows, it adds to the Elephant's perception of you as an accomplished business partner.

Practice helps. The better your act, the more you grow into it. Think Elephant; act Elephant; be Elephant, through and through.

What to Know About Elephants

Who, How, What, and When

Large companies are mysterious entities. Their processes are largely hidden from view. Decisions to buy a product or service typically come about through a series of meetings during which a company representative collects information from you. Then, depending on the circumstances, this information is meshed with company policies and other criteria to determine whether you are the ideal supplier for the company's needs.

Here are the four things you must take into account in order to navigate this process effectively. I recommend reading the entire chapter now, then going back and studying each factor until you are completely comfortable with it.

Know Who Does What

If you believe the person you're dealing with is the only one who decides whether you get the deal, you're probably missing something. You must seek to identify all your constituents at the company and what each needs and expects from you.

Who Influences? The people you're most likely to meet in a company—the marketing manager, purchasing manager, senior buyer, and procurement director, to name a few—are probably information gatherers and influencers, not decision makers. That doesn't make them any less important. Without the influencers' support, you'll never get your proposal in front of the real buyer. Remember that the influencers, like everyone else, want to impress their superiors, so make sure they won't regret plugging you. Help them promote you. Ask and understand the criteria the buyer will use to choose between you and your competitors.

> Once you know who the real buyer or decision maker is, do your best to get to know him. People too often shy away from the powerful, but remember, you have nothing to lose. A quick peek into the office for a handshake and introduction is all it takes. There's no reason to be intimidated. After all, it's you, not the buyer, who owns a business.

Who Buys? These are the people who make the final decision. If you don't have access to them (and you probably don't), you must learn what they value and how you can make them more inclined to give you their business. Part of your task is to ensure that the influencers can present your facts to the buyer in the best possible light. As time goes on, you'll learn through your influencer exactly which hot buttons to push for the specific project you're quoting. For example, should you emphasize cost or product quality? Knowing the answer might mean the difference between a nice sale and a nice try.

Of course, none of this matters if you don't even know who the buyer is. In most cases, you can find out simply by asking the influencers who else is involved in the decision.

Who Kills? Always remember that whatever the merits of your business, someone at the client company can kill the deal without your ever knowing why or who. Keep your ears open for comments your contact may make about the people she is dealing with internally. More likely than not, a casual reference or an outright innuendo will reveal a stumbling block you'll need to be aware of. You can also come right out and ask your contact or potential customer if the purchasing department or some other division or person might kill the deal. If all this sounds a bit like juggling, then you're on the right track. You'll need to manage these potential deal killers.

At P&G, the consumer affairs department has deal-killing powers beyond what I ever would have imagined. It can red-flag any activity that it fears might cause negative consumer feedback. As a matter of policy and courtesy, many marketing brand managers at the company run ideas by the CA department, which handles consumer complaints, among other things.

Once the importance of CA had been explained to me by my contact, I did what I could to develop our relationship. First, I made an appointment with the head of the department and asked her if I could present all our programs to her staff. I wanted her to understand what we were trying to do in case a consumer called with a question or comment. This hour-long meeting gained us incredible mileage. My own consumer relations director went on to work hand-in-hand with her to develop a protocol to handle such calls. The CA department championed us every chance it got—after all, we had acknowledged the staff's importance, given them the respect they deserved, and helped them deal with consumer complaints, their biggest irritation.

Know How to Get on the List

More and more companies try to contract only with vendors or service providers on a preferred vendor list. They do this for several reasons, which vary in importance from company to company:

- To optimize their cost savings by virtue of their size.
- To avoid using vendors who are unreliable or who deliver low-quality goods or services.
- To make their buying process more efficient by reducing the time employees spend making purchases.
- To weed out fraudulent or financially unstable vendors.

If the company maintains a preferred vendor list, make sure your name is at the top, and in as many categories as possible. At P&G, for example, the purchasing department runs a core-supplier program that evaluates potential suppliers on such criteria as pricing, capabilities, and financial strength. It's a brutal process—especially for small businesses, many of whom simply get worn down and just give up and ignore the policy. Although such suppliers may be thrown the occasional scrap of business by a manager unaware of the policy, in the end they do themselves a disservice by trying to buck the purchasing department, which usually squelches the possibility of their winning any significant business.

If your potential client has an approved vendor program, embrace it as a way to separate yourself from your competitors.

As a rule, if your potential client has an approved vendor program or something comparable, embrace it as a way to separate yourself from your competitors. Simply ask your contact or the purchasing department whether the company has a procurement program of some type for your industry. They will be glad to explain the policy and send you the necessary forms. In many cases they are legally required to do so in order to ensure fairness.

Try to meet the person who runs the program; it's always harder for him to say no to someone he's met in person. After introducing myself to P&G's purchasing contact, I asked how the company's core-supplier process worked. She told me that the chief function of the purchasing department was to leverage P&G's formidable size and buying power into cost savings.

Once I understood this goal, I finessed my approach. I explained to her our own Cost Savings Identification Program. Minor detail: I created this program (and its impressive acronym) just days before the meeting. "C-SIP," I explained, would track all the savings we would generate for the P&G brands our company would promote, based on the difference between our regular pricing and the reduced price we would offer as a core supplier. By having a procedure in place and agreeing to put this in a report, we showed the purchasing official exactly what we were bringing to the table.

The point here, of course, isn't the merits of my improvised "C-SIP," but how to understand the needs of company officials. My purchasing contact at P&G needed to prove to her higher-ups that she was saving the company money—and I demonstrated how swift approval of our core-supplier status would do just that. She might just as easily have said that the purpose of her company's core-supplier process was to ensure quality or to weed out financially risky vendors—in which case I would have tailored my pitch to address those concerns, perhaps by describing my company's "QUAD (Quality Assurance Dynamic)" program.

If you can sell a prospect on using your services and he supports you in the procurement program, you have a much better chance for success.

Get a sponsor or champion within the company. This is a great way to give yourself a leg up on your competitors. If you can sell a prospect on using your services and he supports you in the procurement program, you have a much better chance for success.

Know the Company's Lingo and Quirks

Every company speaks its own language—unique acronyms, report names, buzzwords, clichés, and nicknames for people and facilities. Your job is to learn it. Why? Because the lingo distinguishes insiders from outsiders. Which do you want to be?

The only way to learn this internal language is to keep your ears open. During meetings, for example, take note of any unusual terms and phrases you hear or see. If you can't divine from context what a term means, casually ask a trusted contact during your next conversation.

Every company has its own policies, practices, and idiosyncrasies. Studying them can only work to your advantage. P&G, for example, would almost never implement a national marketing program without first conducting a small-scale test to determine whether the proposed sales device would induce consumers to buy the product. The company was very particular about market research, all of which had to be performed by vendors approved by Procter & Gamble.

Many marketing types clamoring for P&G's business weren't aware of this unofficial policy. Some of our competitors would put together tests without the proper P&G-approved market research, or worse, design national programs they could never sell to P&G because they hadn't been pre-tested. We made sure market research was a part of all our test programs. We formed an alliance with a P&G-approved market research firm and worked hard to have as many tests as possible running each year.

> After calling on Procter & Gamble for six months, I felt as if I needed a P&G-to-English dictionary, so I started filling a notepad with translations: "Exhibit 5" was a standard contract, "Blaze" was the code name for a new product, "Central" was headquarters, "The Towers" the connecting building, and so forth.

Know the Budget Season

This might be Basic Sales 101, but it's worth mentioning. Every large company—your client base—develops an annual budget, a process that can take up to three months and sap the energy of many of the company's departments.

An annual budget cycle typically has five distinct phases. For the Elephant you're interested in pitching, you need to learn the details of its budget cycle. Why is this important? If you don't provide the company with the information it needs at the right time, you can easily find yourself locked out of the budget for as much as an entire year. The budget also determines the time when funds are released. If a plan calls for an activity to occur late in the year, the funds will not be released until later in the year, when they are actually needed.

Most of the time, a budget earmarks monies for certain functions but doesn't get into the specifics. To learn the specifics, you need to know when to step on the merry-go-round—that is, to know the start and stop dates of each phase and other details of the company's budget cycle.

Here are a couple of easy ways to get this information. When you are talking about your product or service, ask the company when it budgets and, more important, when it makes the budget decisions relevant to your product, which may be a different time. If the prospective client is a publicly

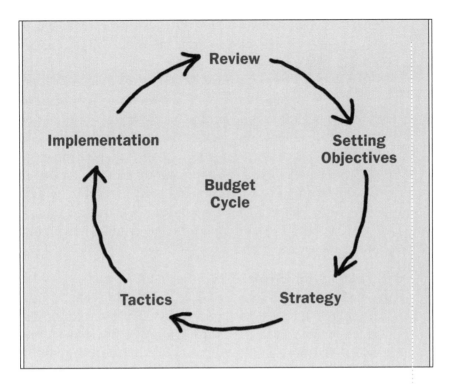

traded company, the annual report (available at the library or through the company's shareholder relations department, often available online) will show when its fiscal year ends—typically December 31, but sometimes June 30 or some other date. You can then guess that the budget season begins about three months earlier.

Regardless of the goods or services you're trying to sell, you can categorize the timing of most of the company's buying decisions as falling into one or more of the budget cycle's phases:

Review. This is the first phase of the budget cycle, and the answers it provides lead directly into the planning or objective-setting phase. Each of the past cycle's business activities is assessed. How did the activity fare? Was it helpful and cost-effective? What worked? What didn't? Which activities will be dropped? Which will be expanded? Which will be altered, and how? These are questions addressed by specialists in market research, auditing, cost analysis, quality control, inventory management, and other areas. If the company outsources any of these services and you wish to provide them, you'll need to have a contract in effect before now; otherwise, all you can get is a small "test" contract.

Regardless of what you sell, it will be evaluated in some manner—and a minor change in the company's operations can have a big impact on your business. Maybe you're selling just one little component, such as polyethylene bags or corporate gifts. These simple items are part of a bigger program. Let's say the polyethylene bags are part of a customer service program, a program that, during review, is found to be ineffective. Guess what? No bags next year. On the other hand, if the program went well and the company doubles its funding, that's great news for you.

Setting objectives. This is the planning phase, in which the business sets its goals and objectives for the coming year. These goals and objectives are conceptually driven by the business owner. Typical sales to this link include consulting services that provide information and advice for the senior company management to use in achieving their objectives. Advertising agencies, marketing consultants, investment companies, legal and accounting services, trend analysts, and other big-picture specialists should try to sell to the big company in this part of the cycle. This means they must approach the Elephant several months to a year before the planning phase in order to be considered.

Strategy. In this phase, the company develops in general terms the means by which the goals and objectives of the business plan are to be achieved. Buying does not usually play a major role in this part of the cycle.

Tactics. The company designs the specific actions to be taken in order to implement the strategies outlined in the previous phase. As in the strategy phase, there are few opportunities for vendors here. However, products and services that may be used during this and other planning phases, such as coffee and catering services to address the needs of participants in long meetings, must be contracted for earlier in the process, typically in the previous cycle's implementation phase. Similarly, if your business is consulting on the design of the big company's strategy and tactics, you've already missed the boat if you make your approach during this phase of the cycle.

Implementation. Now we're getting to the heart of the buying season, when the company implements the strategies it has designed to achieve its goals, and in the process, begins to purchase the products and services it needs to carry out those actions. To do so, it buys everything from coffee for the coffee cart to printing supplies to gifts for customers to advertising programs to packaging. The company also conducts research and analysis to provide data for the review phase and the beginning of the next cycle. About 80 percent of the company's spending occurs in this phase.

Knowledge Is Power

Understanding these four imperatives puts you head and shoulders above others trying to sell to the same big customer. Futility is selling to someone you assume has the authority to give the go-ahead, only to find out later that she was only gathering information. Worse—you didn't even have input into what message was passed along to the decision maker. This happens every day—but no longer to you!

Embracing the Bureaucracy

Making Their Red Tape Work for You

What do you dislike the most about dealing with large companies? Bureaucracy, right? Fighting your way through the red tape of a typical corporation's floor-to-ceiling organization chart maze can be one of the most frustrating aspects of running a business.

My advice to you, however, is to learn to view a big prospect's bureaucracy as a tool you can turn to your advantage. The key is to figure out how it works. If you master its intricacies, you gain insights that can put you well ahead of the competition in bagging and handling the Elephant. It's like having access to all the steam tunnels and ventilation ducts and knowing whose offices they lead to. (No, I wouldn't advise doing what you're thinking.)

After you've learned to navigate in a few large companies, you'll find yourself scanning the horizon for the next bureaucracy the way a surfer looks for the biggest, gnarliest wave. You can use it to launch your sales and profits into orbit. You can also help your big-company customer simplify and improve its own processes—thus making yourself even more useful to your client and bolstering your long-term prospects.

Learn the System

A bureaucracy, in all its complexity, is the software that keeps a giant company running, a control system with built-in fail-safe routines designed to avoid catastrophe. It funnels every decision through a gauntlet of decision makers to ensure that prescribed standards of quality and cost are maintained. By its very nature and purpose, it slows things down and lowers operating efficiency—but it's a necessary evil. (In fact, having been an Elephant myself, I have known the joys of owning my own bureaucracy.)

> **Having been an Elephant myself, I have known the joys of owning my own bureaucracy.**

When you approach a big company with an eye for doing business with it, get an early start toward understanding its bureaucracy. Study it, map it, look for its hidden connections and patterns.

Analyze activity. Study every activity inside your prospect company. What processes do its managers routinely use to get approvals? Who do they have to talk to? How do they interact with their other departments? What forms do they fill out? How is information communicated to you? Knowing the answers to these questions can mean windfalls for you.

Try to understand their processes, then find ways to exploit each link in the process chain for streamlining opportunities. If you can streamline a process, or perhaps simplify the requirements of the person constrained by the process, you can create a money-making opportunity.

Review correspondence. When you get letters, e-mails, even signed contracts, pay attention to who's included on the routing—their names are there for a reason. Find out their titles and departments. This will give you greater insight into how best to integrate your business into the mix. For example, if you notice that people from the customer's production, quality control, and public relations departments are included on correspondence, make it a point to meet them. Ask them how you can help them with respect to your proposal or contract. Try to uncover the main issues they have with suppliers in your industry, and work to develop processes that will reassure them your business won't give them the same problems.

Perfect Your Processes

Quite often you will see that your Elephant's bureaucratic processes are not suitable for your business–they add cost, unnecessarily complicate your business activities, or even threaten the quality of your product or service. How do you sidestep this destructive kind of bureaucratic interference?

Regardless of whether you have 2 or 200 employees, the answer is to fight process with process. In fact, the fewer employees you have, the more important it is to convey processes to the Elephant. This is easy to do, and it will put you light-years ahead of your competitors. When selling to decision makers in a bureaucracy, don't make vague promises about how you'll meet their needs; explain your processes in detail. This will reassure them that the activity will occur.

Most of these processes can be quite simple. Here are a couple that I used in my businesses:

- Cost savings analysis outlined for the customer just how much money they were saving from quantity discounting by giving my company more and more business.
- Logistics sheets provided a quick and easy 100-foot view of all my current activities with the big customer. This was helpful to the many support departments that were usually left out of the loop and who, in turn, loved my company because we kept them in the know.

In my businesses, I made a point of creating processes, giving them a brand name, and promoting them in my sales literature. All sales and account people would use them regularly in sales calls, proposals, and presentations. For example, our process for proving that our product samples actually reached the hands of the intended customers was called "SampleTrack," and our research-matching process was "Accumatch." I had about fifty different processes, each focusing on a customer need or a claim from my company. These were branded and promoted to give the client a sense of their importance to us—but mostly they were created to give comfort to the big customers.

Tune Up Your Elephant

Surprise! You're not the only one who's fed up with red tape. So are many of the folks at your Elephant.

Remember, a big company's bureaucracy is a functional, although often frustrating, necessity. However, it may be more complex and tangled than it needs to be—and that's where you can make yourself a hero to your big-company customer.

My advice is to view the bureaucracy that enables the company to chug along every day as an opportunity—an opportunity to help your clients survive their own bureaucracy. I'd even go so far as to say that over the years my company's ability to analyze, adapt, and apply big-business bureaucracy to our advantage has netted us several million dollars.

Your potential client probably doesn't like dealing with the internal bureaucracy any more than you do—and she has to live with it every day.

Your potential client probably doesn't like dealing with the internal bureaucracy any more than you do—and she has to live with it every day. Help her. When she takes your information to fill out her own company's never-ending forms, ask her how her company plans to use your data so you can give it to her in a useful format.

For example, my company had different proposal layouts for different prospects. One client's company required her to run a detailed cost analysis on the information gleaned from suppliers like us. We took it upon ourselves to actually run the numbers and gave her everything she needed as part of our proposal, in the correct format, so that all she needed do was pass along the proposal with a cost analysis. She loved this so much that she gave us tons of projects—simply because we did her work.

Here's another example: Our marketing programs for P&G distributed trial-size product samples to specific target audiences, typically kids, teens, or college students. P&G officials weren't sure how they should monitor the delivery of the samples to our many scattered packing facilities because we used so many different ones to try to lower costs—as many as thirty, unlike most of our competitors, who used just one.

Working with the production staff at P&G, my vice president developed a simple form that each packer could use to record how many samples it received. The packers e-mailed us the forms for easy consolidation into a master record, which we forwarded to our contact at P&G's shipping department. Problem solved—and the benefit to us was that the customer paid for the long-haul shipping of the product samples. This lowered our shipping costs considerably.

Another time, we had trouble with our matching panels—a market-research term meaning two contrasting groups of people under study. In our case, one group consisted of people targeted by a marketing program; the other group had the same demographic profile but would not receive the program. The goal was to compare the responses from the two groups to determine whether the marketing program was inspiring people to buy the product.

Matching the panels was tedious. I was amazed to learn that, even in such a sophisticated company, the matching process hadn't been automated through custom software. Pencil and paper and spreadsheets was the only option, one that took weeks. Even worse, once the matching was complete, if a consumer slated to receive the program dropped out, the panels would become "unmatched" and they'd be back to square one.

Another big opportunity had arisen. To seize it, we worked with P&G's market research department to develop the first automated panel-matching software. We were able to shorten the matching process from several weeks to several minutes. We realized millions of dollars in increased sales because we could now provide solid data on how effective our marketing programs were. Another bonus: since we developed and

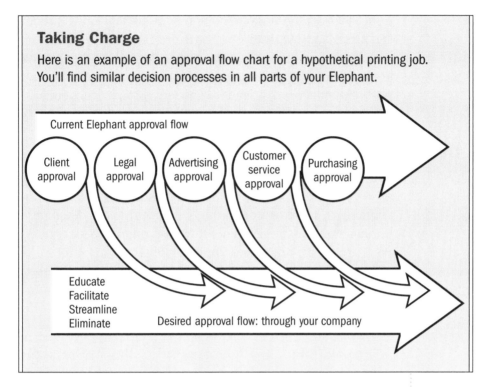

Taking Charge

Here is an example of an approval flow chart for a hypothetical printing job. You'll find similar decision processes in all parts of your Elephant.

Current Elephant approval flow

Client approval

Legal approval

Advertising approval

Customer service approval

Purchasing approval

Educate
Facilitate
Streamline
Eliminate

Desired approval flow: through your company

essentially owned the software, we became even closer to P&G as well as many other companies.

Hijack the Elephant's Processes

The chart above shows part of a bureaucratic process chain that might occur inside your Elephant for, say, approval of a print job for which you have submitted a proposal. Each step of the process requires signatures from one or more of the managers that make up the bureaucracy. If you, as the printer, truly know and understand this chain, you can take control of the Elephant's bureaucracy—that is, you can get the Elephant to let you take over much of its bureaucratic process flow. Here's how:

Educate yourself on exactly how, what, and who is involved with each step in the approval chain. As you learned in "Know Who Does What" in the previous chapter, sometimes the "who" is the most important thing to know. It's not just the decision maker of record; sometimes what you think is a done deal can be undone by someone further downstream. It's also highly valuable to know the people who influence the decision makers and deal killers. Work with them; make yourself familiar and useful to them. The more you become part of their process, the more you will gain control of it.

Facilitate the Elephant's progress from link to link, ideally by participating in each phase. When you first go through the process, everything is done by the client; you are expected to wait to receive the film or disk for printing. Think of this not as idle time but as an opportunity. Rather than accepting the status quo, work at integrating yourself into the Elephant's bureaucracy. Learn how each of these approvals is granted, who grants it, and what that person's criteria are. Once you understand this machinery in its parts and its entirety and can help your client with the gritty details, you can become indispensable—because your client probably hates the company's bureaucratic processes even more than you do.

Streamline the process for the various links. For example, once you know that customer service has specific things it looks for (such as including the company's toll-free number in an ad or "Address Correction Requested" on a mailer), you can help your client remember these details to guarantee there will be no snags in getting customer service's approval. Create a checklist covering all of the Elephant's important and mandatory process requirements. This will go far in easing their concerns about giving you a larger role in their process.

Once you've got your foot in the door, set up a meeting with the customer service folks to introduce yourself. Over time you should be able to establish direct processes that let you act as the link between your client and the Elephant's other departments. You might need to get people in your own company to "infiltrate" the other departments, but that will be even more helpful in dealing with future clients inside the Elephant. I used to do this all the time, and I can tell you from personal experience that it was remarkably successful. Once the linked departments felt comfortable that I knew what I was doing, they couldn't wait to release the approval link to me.

Eliminate unnecessary processes. Although you'll never replace some departments in the process chain, such as legal, you should try to own the communication between your client and as many of the Elephant's departments as possible—to be the facilitator of as many decisions as possible in the process chains that are most important to you. When you do this, all of these departments become, in effect, your clients, each of which will recommend you to new departments, new clients. You'll be amazed at how much business this will get you.

Part III

ROMANCING
YOUR ELEPHANT

Drawing Up
Your Hit List

Finding Your Best Big-Company Prospects

Okay, you've got your mind right. Your entire business has got the big-customer focus. Everybody's ready to go out and bag an Elephant. Now what?

Now's the time to decide *which* Elephant. There's not much point to setting out blindly in search of an unnamed giant company. There are only so many years in a century.

Although your business could potentially sell to many big customers, not all big customers are right for you. You need to focus on the Elephants you're most likely to bag—and to develop a mutually beneficial, long-term relationship with.

Your next step is to position your product or service for the big customer. After that, you will develop a hit list of big companies you believe might make good customers for what you provide, as well as good partners for your own business. Once you've compiled this list, you'll need to whittle it down to the best of the best. That's what this chapter is about.

We'll start with something that's fun to do.

Positioning Your Business

Here's an exercise that will stimulate your brain: write down all the different ways you can think of that your products or services might be useful to big customers. Look at your business from the perspective of the big company. Does this change your view of your product or service? Can the customer use it as it is? Would it be more useful if it were modified? Write down everything that comes to mind.

When you think of big customers, look beyond the obvious contenders. If you traditionally target the general public, for example, consider adapting your product for businesses. Think broadly about potential clients. If you're a self-employed plumber, consider local businesses, such as contractors and builders, that might expand your client base and attract referrals. If you own a bowling alley complete with video arcades and party rooms, consider companies that could use your space for meetings or team-building activities.

Five Steps in Positioning Your Business

1. Listing your revenue streams.

2. Identifying and listing your operational mandates.

3. Initial Elephant positioning.

4. Big-customer research.

5. Putting it all together.

To gain a better understanding of these steps, see "Five Steps to Position for Success" in the Free Resources link at www.differencemaker.com.

Also, take another look at the list of businesses in the table on page 14. How have these businesses positioned themselves for the big customer?

Thinking along these lines will not only expand your hit list but give you ideas for increasing revenues as well. Remember to review this activity as you start to learn more and more about what big companies need and how they operate.

Compiling Your Hit List

Make a long list of all potential big customers you can think of. Be as outrageous as you can, but match the companies with the need they might have for what you provide—that is, list exactly how you could help them. Never overlook the obvious prospects. Sometimes the best prospects—companies that might spend a lot of money on whatever product or service you provide—are right under your nose. If you sell specialty foods, for example, Neiman Marcus could be your answer. And don't ignore smaller companies that are growing fast and showing signs of becoming true Elephants; a friend made on the way up the ladder together can be a friend for life.

When my marketing business was still young, I knew that because our product was expensive we had to find large national companies with generous marketing budgets. I remember going to the library and poring over the *Standard Directory of Advertisers,* the bible of the advertising and marketing industry. I listed every company that met my criteria, including Kraft Foods, Unilever, Johnson & Johnson, Johnson Wax, Quaker Oats, Helene Curtis, Warner Lambert, and, of course, Procter & Gamble.

> **Don't ignore smaller companies that are growing fast and showing signs of becoming true Elephants; a friend made on the way up the ladder together can be a friend for life.**

Selecting the Best Target

Once you've scoured the business landscape for the obvious prospects, the less obvious ones, and the downright imaginative possibilities, it's time to carve out a realistic list of the most promising, however few.

At this point, you obviously don't know all you need to know about your prospects. Below are five questions you should ask, along with some examples and explanations that should help narrow your search. Go through each company on your list and rank your prospects according to how they fare with these questions:

Q: Which prospects have the most to spend on your product or service?

Most industries and their associations publish resources like the *Standard Directory of Advertisers* that readily provide this type of information. The reasoning behind this question is obvious: you want to know who has the big bucks.

Information, Please

These are some of the resources I use to obtain the information necessary to answer my questions about prospective big companies and narrow my list:

- Industry publications can be found either online, at the library, or by contacting the relevant industry association. If you're unaware of any associations in your industry, ask around, take a trip to the local public library and ask at the reference desk for assistance, or run an online search by "(industry name)" + "association."

- Annual survey guides published by industry or the government can be helpful if your prospect is a public company or a government agency. Details of government and important industry spending—those that affect economic forecasting indicators such as the GNP, unemployment, and retail spending—are often published and available through your public library or the Internet. Search online under "(industry)" + "annual survey."

- Industry and company spending guides are typically published annually by industry magazines, which you can contact. And keep your eyes peeled when you visit your prospect's lobby; these publications are often left lying around the lobby.

- Rankings of the largest companies and industry spending by company are published annually by industry associations and are found in special issues of their publications. One of the best known such lists is the Fortune 500, compiled by *Fortune* magazine.

- Annual reports and mission statements are available via the Web or, for public companies, by request from shareholder relations.

- Input from sales forces and competitors is important because it provides a unique firing-line perspective. However, keep in mind that individuals base their comments on their own experiences (and personalities and axes to grind), so speak with several sources before generalizing.

- Information about how the prospect evaluates business proposals is a bit more difficult to come by. Probably the only way you can get this information is through a friendly competitor who has worked with the prospect. Once you make contact and find the prospect wants a proposal, you can ask directly.

Q: Does the prospect's business philosophy dovetail with your strengths?

A large, prosperous company can be an appealing target, but remember that the relationship will fail if you're a poor match. In hindsight, I know that my own company often spent too much time wooing incompatible clients. We specialized in long-term marketing programs that required eighteen months or more to achieve their results. Yet we used to pair up with brand managers whose senior management based success solely on twelve-month performance—too short a time for our product to work its magic.

Procter & Gamble, by contrast, sought long-term customer loyalty by persuading consumers to buy its brands and then focusing on keeping them as customers for the rest of their lives—a focus that complemented my own company's approach quite well. (For more insights into Procter & Gamble and other enduring companies, check out *Built to Last: Successful Habits of Visionary Companies,* by James Collins and Jerry Porras.)

Q: How does the prospect reward the employees who would be buying your product or services?

On what basis do the buyers at your prospective client receive bonuses and promotions? Are they evaluated according to their ability to bring innovative ideas to the table, to buy at the lowest possible price, to enhance the company image, to increase total company profits, or by some other criterion? The answer can help you determine whether your company fits the client's incentive structure. For example, if your product carries a premium price tag and the company you're considering bases employee bonuses solely on the ability to buy at the lowest price, expect a tough road ahead.

Q: How much does the company really need you?

Avoid the impulse to respond, "A lot." Put yourself in the prospect's shoes. Are the company's competitors making headway in an arena where you can help it succeed? Does the number-two company in the industry need your help in gaining ground more than the number-one company needs you to increase its lead? Is your product or service vital to its operations, or is it merely a nice add-on?

Q: How far afield will the association lead you?

You should also consider the logistics of the big company. Note which prospects are convenient to your business. All else being equal, why not stay local? I wouldn't base my decision solely on logistics, but in a tossup I'd choose a handy location.

As you review and rank your prospects, a few of them will creep to the top of your list. They're your first targets—companies that have money to spend on your type of services, subscribe to a business philosophy that plays to your strengths, and reward their buyers in a manner consistent with how you operate. Now comes the hard part—convincing the prospects that you're right for them, too.

Knocking on Doors

Making That First Solid Contact

Now that you've identified target companies and understand generally how large companies operate and the best ways to approach them, it's time to get to work. I'll take you step-by-step through my approach to winning big clients. I've personally used this method many times and have recommended it to others with good success. (A reminder: unless you've read the whole book and understood the strategy of selling to big customers, this chapter won't be very helpful to you.)

The goal here isn't just to set meetings, it's to land that big client. The New Client Development Flow Chart (opposite) shows the process at a glance.

Step 1: Building Your Prospect Database

Your first task is to generate a list of specific people to contact at your prospective companies. Don't feel dismayed or overwhelmed—you can

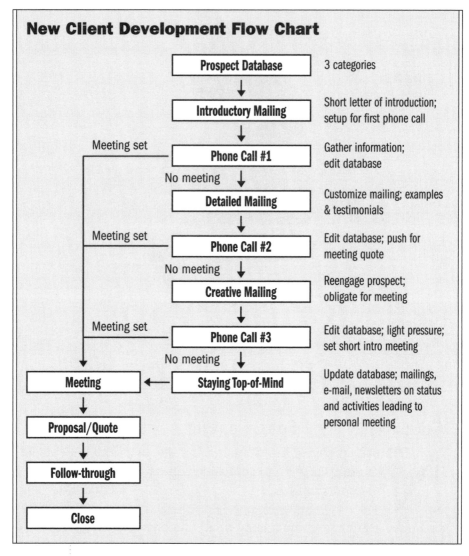

New Client Development Flow Chart

Prospect Database	3 categories
Introductory Mailing	Short letter of introduction; setup for first phone call
Phone Call #1	Gather information; edit database
Detailed Mailing	Customize mailing; examples & testimonials
Phone Call #2	Edit database; push for meeting quote
Creative Mailing	Reengage prospect; obligate for meeting
Phone Call #3	Edit database; light pressure; set short intro meeting
Staying Top-of-Mind → **Meeting**	Update database; mailings, e-mail, newsletters on status and activities leading to personal meeting
Proposal/Quote	
Follow-through	
Close	

Meeting set — Phone Call #1 / Phone Call #2 / Phone Call #3
No meeting — Detailed Mailing / Creative Mailing / Staying Top-of-Mind

develop the list systematically even when you're starting with a blank slate. Be imaginative, resourceful, and tenacious. You have nothing to lose; you probably won't get to see most of these people anyway.

Meghan and Emily, co-owners of Touching Memories Custom Stationery, captured leads by looking through company annual reports. They sought out the human resources directors at several companies and were off to the races. They called high-level directors, who were only too happy to pass along the names of mid-level and lower-level employees, who turned out to be the sisters' most fruitful contacts.

I've used this strategy myself. I'd call a prospect's main number and ask to speak with the VP of marketing or whatever, knowing full well that I'd be transferred to the VP's assistant instead. I'd muster up all my charm, big-time nice, and plead for help. I'd play dumb and ask if she could be so kind as to suggest contacts I could send information about my company. I'd make a point of asking for the names and extensions of managers in different divisions, figuring they'd be widely scattered in the corporate complex and thus served by different administrators, increasing my chances of success.

Then I would start dialing. During each initial contact I would seek another name to add to my list, which I updated each evening. I'd be sure to contact that name and expand my list, and so forth. In two days I'd have made 150 calls and acquired a database of some 75 prospects, an encouraging start. Once you begin meeting with potential clients, it becomes even easier to generate more prospects.

Be Kind to Your Database

Keep your database fresh and work diligently to increase its size. Mailing to people who are no longer with a company is a waste of money. Use software to keep your database current. The software must enable you to perform mail merges to generate letters or labels and also let you track data such as hobbies, family, and lead-potential rating— so that, for example, you can print out a list of your hot leads.

Often your potential client will bring associates to your meeting. Write down the names of anyone attending the meeting not already in your database, regardless of rank.

If you get a chance to walk down the halls with your prospective client, jot down as many names as possible from cubicle or office nameplates. When you get back to your own office, call the main number and ask for each person's title and extension number. If the receptionist refuses, ask to be connected; people often leave their titles on their voice mail greetings, and you never know which of them might pick up their phones. Corporate Web sites sometimes supply this information as well.

Once you establish a relationship at the company, try to get a copy of the company directory. Some companies are willing to share this information.

Then, as you get new prospects, divide them into three categories:

Hot leads. You know the company or division buys what you sell and are sure the contact name you have is a good one.

Great fits. Even if the company or division isn't buying what you're selling, you're convinced that it should be.

Secondary leads. The prospect isn't in the market to buy your product right now, but you want to introduce your business to him all the same.

Step 2: Introductory Mailing

Objective: To quickly introduce yourself and your business.

Write a cover letter, about two-thirds of a page, that shows off what you do. If need be, include a promotional sheet with more detail, but keep the letter clean and clutter-free. To keep it from looking like a form letter, buy software that will print names and data into the body of your letters. Remember, you're not expecting to get an order here—you're trying to build credibility and top-of-mind awareness as you set the stage for a phone call and later mailings.

If you're strapped for cash, as I was, target these materials to the hot leads and great fits, foregoing the secondary leads for now. Remember to delete from the database the names from any returned mailings.

One business I owned a while back needed to get an introductory mailing out, but funds were so tight that we couldn't even afford brochures. I had to improvise. I went to the drugstore and bought a bunch of those cheap walnut-looking folders. I asked a local graphic artist to create some rub-ons with my business's name. To save on printing costs, my six employees and I used quarters to rub the business name onto each folder. Glamorous it wasn't, but it did the job.

Step 3: Phone Call #1

When: Two or three days after your prospects have presumably received the introductory mailing.

Objectives: To gather information necessary for future contacts and to set up a meeting to present your products or services to a legitimate buyer.

Before you pick up the phone, prepare a script, or at least some bullet points. Practice with one of your employees or even your spouse, and then with some calls to prospects who don't matter, before calling the ones who really count.

Mention your mailing and your product. If the conversation flows naturally and the prospect appears to have been favorably impressed by the mailing, set up a meeting right then and there. More likely, you won't get this far, so remember that the goal here is simply to gather information for your next contact. Use this initial contact to learn as much as you can about your prospect, but don't hang on like a leech; the last thing you want people to feel is that you're pushy or long-winded.

During your initial phone contact, try to get answers to the following questions for your records. If appropriate, you might even take the next step and ask to provide a price quote.

- What would the prospect expect to see in a product or service like yours?
- Is your prospect someone who buys, influences, kills, or does something else altogether?
- From whom does her company currently buy comparable products, and is it happy with those relationships?
- What unique opportunities might there be with this prospect? You might find that the prospect's company wants to expand its supplier base, has a sudden need for your services, or is bringing out a new product or service you can help with.

Get organized. Before you start calling potential clients, get your house in order. If you're doing things right, the phone should be stuck to your ear, which will make it harder to keep all the information straight. I suggest using a contact sheet to help organize new client activity.

Every day at my company, I'd start at the top of the list and hit the phones, attempting to call each entry until I reached the last one on the last page. Then I'd start over. There were many days when I'd make five or six attempts before actually speaking with the prospect. Other days I'd call and call but never make contact. Since I never left messages, they didn't know the level of my tenacity or think of me as a pest.

After each contact I made, I'd jot down the results in the appropriate section of the report. If I reached the contact directly, I'd also note the time of the call. Human beings are creatures of habit, so if you're able to get through to someone at a specific time, you can probably reach the same person at the same time on a different day.

Make sure to keep up with the "status/action needed" columns. Using a computer-based form can make these tasks easier.

Prospect Contact Sheet

Contact sheets come in many shapes and sizes. Here's what's across the top of the contact sheet I like to use:

1. Name
2. Phone number
3. Department
4. Fax number
5. Business
6. Mailing #1
7. Phone call #1 (time)
8. Status/action needed
9. Mailing #2
10. Phone call #2 (time)
11. Status/action needed
12. Mailing #3
13. Phone call #3 (time)
14. Status/action needed

Step 4: Detailed Mailing

When: Immediately after contacting the prospect (step 3), but in any event no more than three days later, even if you're including price quotes.

Objectives: To give the prospect detailed information about your services and to set up a meeting to present what you have to offer.

Customize this detailed mailing, starting with a one-page cover letter tailored to each prospect, based on what you learned during your initial phone call (step 3). Include features that will showcase your business and appeal to the prospect—testimonials, brochures, work samples, or any other proof that your product or service stands out. Resist the urge to send too much; better to forward a thin envelope than to burden the prospect with extraneous material. If you're not sure what to say or do at this juncture, then you probably didn't do an adequate job of gathering information during step 3.

I always like to add a personal touch to my letters by including a handwritten line or adding a Post-it note. I do this to humanize the process a bit and remind the recipient that an actual person is on the other end of the exchange.

Step 5: Phone Call #2

When: Two days after the prospect has received the detailed mailing (step 4).

Objectives: To set up a meeting in which you can present your services to a potential buyer, and to further develop your relationship.

This time, you'll have sent along enough information to give your prospect a working understanding of what you do. Typically, fewer than half of the recipients will actually look at your materials. Of those, only a fraction will pass your materials along to someone else—and the rest will look for the trash can. Think of it this way: it's still a numbers game. As long as your prospecting was sound, you'll have more than enough potential customers to keep you busy.

The goal here is to set up a meeting to highlight your business and convince the prospect that your product or service is indispensable. Refer to the information you've collected, remind her of your initial call, and, if appropriate, mention specific items in your mailing.

Feel out the contact. If you can, grab an hour slot. More likely, you'll meet some resistance. Never ask if she wants to meet. It's far more effective to say, "I'll be in your area on Tuesday and need only fifteen minutes of your time. How's ten o'clock?" Then keep the meeting to fifteen minutes. You

Phone Tips

Relax. The telephone gives you some tremendous advantages. Because no one can see you, you can glance at notes or work virtually anywhere that you're comfortable. Take care to develop an upbeat and cheerful phone demeanor. Most of all, get comfortable with the device.

Off time. Many of your potential clients will be hard to reach during a typical nine-to-five day. Many, however, come in early or stay late. Since their assistants aren't there to block your calls at those times, you have a better chance of getting through. I experienced the best results between 7:30 and 8:30 am and from 5:30 to 7:00 pm.

No voice mails. Sometimes I wonder if voice mail was invented to ruin salespeople's lives. I have a hard-and-fast rule on voice mails for new prospects: don't leave them, ever. Because people really don't know who you are, 99.9 percent of them won't call you back, and all you'll accomplish is to look desperate. Even worse, if you do leave voice mail, you bar yourself from calling them back, at least for a few days. Voice mail lobs the ball into their court, where you don't want it, for if they don't feel like playing with you, you're out of luck.

Call until you drop. As I said before, I made up to 150 calls a day. (I talked on the phone so much at work that I began to hate talking on the phone at home.) I urge you to list of all your prospective clients on the contact sheets and get started top to bottom—then rinse and repeat. As soon as you get someone on the phone, talk about your most recent mailing.

No weather checks. Always call for a reason, not just to "touch base." Announce relevant new activities in your business, or ask whether your contact

can push, but not too hard. Remember that you're in this for the long haul. There will be more meetings coming up, and you'll soon be sending out a more detailed mailing. You might have more luck waiting until then to press harder.

Step 6: Creative Mailing

When: Two weeks after phone call #2 (step 5) for prospects who haven't yet agreed to meet with you.

Objectives: To find creative ways to re-engage the prospect and persuade him to agree to a meeting.

received your mailing. Having a purpose matters even more when you've met with a client and need to find out, without coming across as a pest, if she's going to buy.

It's a numbers game. If you're fully committed and are working a sound plan, you'll probably succeed. Along the way, however, you'll surely experience a lot of rejection and frustration. Understand that it's all a numbers game—the more calls you make, the better your chances. Many people become discouraged with the rejection and simply stop calling. Don't fall into that trap.

Silence is golden. A common error is failure to tolerate silence during a phone call. Typically, the prospect wavers about whether to set up a meeting or commit to a sale, and in the meantime, you get tense about the silence at the other end of the line. Resist the urge to dispel the tension by spouting something like, "Why don't you think about it and let me know tomorrow?" You'd only be letting him off the hook.

Always go for the close. Once you've made your initial contact, do whatever it takes to realize your goal, whether it be a meeting, referral, sale, or something else. You can soft sell or hard sell, depending on your personality and the situation, but even if your prospect isn't quite ready to commit, use the call to prepare for the next one. Figure out what's making her hesitate, do your best to fix or work around the hitch, and get back to her.

Be real. At times it's appropriate to throw in the towel. If you're convinced that further discussions with a contact will be fruitless, change his status to secondary lead and spend your time targeting prospects with more potential. But whatever you do, don't throw in the towel simply because you've run into a little resistance.

You've already sent two mailings to your prospects and have spoken to them at least once, and—lo and behold—they're proving hard to crack. It's time for a less traditional mailing that appeals to people's lighter side and sense of humor.

The creative mailing is more of an advertisement for your business than a hard sell for your product. You've already sent the company relevant information and letters focusing on its needs. Now it's time to employ an unusual hook.

I used to sell Halloween safety programs to schools, and one September I sent principals mini-pumpkins with stickers bearing the name of my company, SCA. Another time, I sent a paperclip holder with "Attach Yourself to SCA" on the side. Yet another time, I sent gourmet taffy apples with a card from SCA that read, "Bite into Your Competitors' Business."

Your goal here is to get prospects to contact you to talk about the gift—or at least be receptive when you call to see if they received it. You'll be surprised how constructively such creativity pays off. For those prospects who now agree to see you, this mailing should break the ice when you first meet.

Remember to choose a mailing piece that has something to do with your business, and don't forget to include contact information in your mailing.

Step 7: Phone Call #3

When: For the prospects with whom you have not set up a meeting, one week after they receive your creative mailing.

Objectives: To set up a prospect meeting, and to further develop the relationship with your prospect nonintrusively.

This time, you're calling primarily to make sure your prospect received the creative mailing. Mention that you're going to be in the area and would love to stop by for a few minutes to introduce yourself. If he agrees, keep your word and stay only five or ten minutes. He'll be impressed that you didn't try to steal more time. On several occasions, clients have told me that they eventually agreed to a formal meeting only because I stayed for precisely the length of time I said I would, a sign that I valued their time.

Step 8: Staying Top-of-Mind

If you haven't secured a meeting or developed the relationship to this point, don't get discouraged. Some relationships take more time to cultivate. In fact, some of the longest client relationships I've maintained took quite a while to develop. One reason is that some prospects are loyal to their suppliers, and unless they have a reason to look elsewhere, they don't. Your job is to be patient, stay the course, wait for your opportunity, and be ready to step in and deliver for your prospect.

This is also a good spot to reevaluate your list, placing each prospect into the appropriate category.

Every few weeks or months, send out an inexpensive mailing to your prospects that features your achievements, new clients, samples of your latest work, or any press you might have received. This will help you keep your company top-of-mind. If money is tight, limit the contact to hot leads and great fits.

Matching the Prospector to the Prospect

Putting Your Best Face Forward

You have an account that's been working well for you for some time. Revenues are strong with this customer, and the staff there seems to genuinely enjoy working with your company. Your salesperson on the account decides to leave and go elsewhere, but you're not that worried, because you believe that she was a bit underqualified and overpaid for such a big account and that the account could yield more if you had a real tiger in there.

To take the reins, you hire an experienced high-level sales professional, a real pro with a great track record. You can tell right away he's a tenacious guy. You can't wait to set him loose on the account.

Several weeks later you receive a call from a very irritated high-level manager at the big customer. You ask what the problem is and are made to understand that you'd better get rid of this guy immediately or the Elephant will walk.

Shocked, you have no choice but to pull the plug, and you do so. You call back and are told that your sales employee was rude and obnoxious.

You talk to the new salesperson. He has no idea what the problem was—he was "just selling." You decide to give him another chance. You put him on a different account. One year later he's your top salesman.

What happened here?

What happened was the simple mistake of putting the wrong personality type in the wrong selling situation. It's a common mistake—and often fatal. In fact, placing the right personality type with the right customer can easily mean the difference between success and failure. The good thing is that matching a salesperson with a company is not hard to master. It's a simple, two-step process:

1. Profile your salesperson.
2. Match him with the company where he'll have the best chance for success.

Profiling Your Sales Personnel

In my experience, salespeople fall into three basic types based on their personalities, styles, and approaches:

- The Sage
- The Pal
- The Pit Bull

Each type can be effective in particular situations. Although some salespeople may seem to fit more than one category, usually one type is dominant. With experience, a salesperson can change from one type to another, especially if she finds a style that better suits her.

The Sage

Who is the Sage? The Sage cites his own experience to make the buyer comfortable with him and his product. He often uses reasoning and a pencil to provide the buyer with irrefutable evidence, then compares his product to the competition's to clinch the deal. Though he may be gregarious at heart, he is most often reserved at work. He succeeds by capitalizing on his experience and knowledge, not from being warm and fuzzy.

Descriptors: Knowledge, experience, comfort, trust.

When the Sage thrives: He's trying to sell to a conscientious or skeptical customer who is concerned about buying the wrong product, doubtful of whether he should be buying it at all, or worried about how he'll look if he makes a poor purchasing decision.

Generally, the Sage likes to be of an age that puts him at the height of his game in his industry. For a sale to a business, for example, the target age might be forties or older. For retail clothing sales in a shopping mall, on the other hand, late teens or twenties might be preferable. Ideally, the Sage is old enough to inspire confidence but young enough not to appear out of touch.

What the Sage needs from you to succeed:

- Useful information, such as examples of what he's done for other clients, case studies, spec sheets, and reference lists.
- Proof of your product's best features, whether through market research, industry or consumer test reports, or sales figures.
- Timely, accurate responses to the customer's questions.

If you have a retail business such as a jewelry store, consider creating a chart for your Sage that he can use to educate customers on the wonderful world of diamonds, putting their minds at ease along the way.

What motivates the Sage: To play to the Sage's strengths in experience and knowledge, ask him to mentor less experienced salespeople, encourage him to pursue education in the field, and find conventions where he can expand his knowledge base.

The Pal

Who is the Pal? The Pal is a great relationship builder. A successful Pal is very outgoing and makes friends easily. She may be light on substance and knowledge about the product, but she has no peer when it comes to linking business with relationships. Customers will buy from the Pal simply because they like her.

Pals are adept at adapting their opinions and small talk to suit their audience. A Pal is the type to rave about a sports team in one conversation, then scorn the same team in the next conversation. Consistency aside, I've had a lot of luck putting Pals on tough accounts where the merits of the business alone couldn't make the sale.

It's important to remember that the main attribute of the Pal is her uncanny ability to build relationships, an invaluable tool in your sales arsenal.

Descriptor: Relationships.

When the Pal thrives: Whenever her customer wants more from a salesperson than business, and especially when the person she's trying to sell to isn't actually making the decision but is simply recommending a supplier. The Pal likes to be in the same peer group as the customer. Pals also thrive when they are able to use entertainment as a sales tool. Clients who are willing and able to take advantage of a free lunch or sporting event should be receptive to the Pal.

What the Pal needs from you to succeed:

- Clear, simple, and detailed materials that explain your product or service. These might include a printed or computer presentation she can memorize or flip charts she can share with potential customers.
- Being paired with a Sage. They can have a positive effect on each other—and more important, on the customer.
- Your consent to spend money on entertainment. Remember to account for this cost in your sales price and financial forecasts.

What motivates the Pal: The Pal lives to interact with other people. Social activities always put a smile on her face; she likes to feel needed and wanted. The Pal genuinely enjoys the customer relationships she has built, and she enjoys receiving praise and credit for the value her people skills bring to the business. These interactions provide much of the Pal's motivation. Acknowledge her ability to forge relationships—for that is the cornerstone to customer loyalty.

The Pit Bull

Who is the Pit Bull? The Pit Bull is all business. He doesn't come to work to make friends, either with co-workers or with sales contacts. Instead, he churns through prospects until he maximizes his sales. It's all a numbers game to the Pit Bull. If he loses an account, so be it—there are more out there. By the same token, the Pit Bull is typically poor at customer service and often loses repeat business as a result. His tenacity breeds

	Sages	**Pals**	**Pit Bulls**
Descriptor	Knowledge Experience Comfort Trust	Relationships	Business Bottom line
When they thrive	Concerned customer Cautious customer	Client seeking friendship Information gatherer Same peer group as customer Client seeking entertainment	Independent accounts Competitive industries Authority to close
What they need	Information Proof of product References Case studies	Help with details Pairing with others Visiting customers Solid sales materials Entertainment budget	Independence Account support Defined pricing Simple closing process
What motivates them	Education Enhanced mentor role	Interactions and relationships in and out of the company	Money Stretched quotas Sales contests

success, but it also creates enemies, both inside and outside the company.

That said, I've seen tremendously successful Pit Bulls in nearly every industry. The trick for you is to sic the Pit Bull onto the right customers. Although the Pit Bull might not mind alienating prospects, you probably will.

Descriptors: Business, the bottom line.

When the Pit Bull thrives: Pit Bulls prosper when they're let off the leash. They appreciate having the latitude they need to clinch deals on the spot. Some good industries for a Pit Bull include real estate, car sales, telemarketing, and stock brokering by phone.

What the Pit Bull needs from you to succeed:

- Independence.
- Enough pricing latitude to close the deal as soon as possible.
- Customer service support, to mitigate the weak points. If appropriate, adjust compensation to account for the added costs.
- A simplified closing process, so he can move on to the next sale.

What motivates the Pit Bull: One word—money. Set targets at a level where he'll have to stretch, but if he reaches the target, make sure he cashes in. A Pit Bull prefers to deal with customers who won't be turned off by his somewhat abrasive style. He wants to be appreciated for his drive, so try not to chastise him every time you get a minor complaint about his personality.

Since Pit Bulls are innately competitive, sales contests can be ideal motivators. It doesn't matter much what the prize is—for the Pit Bull, winning is what counts.

Square Peg in the Square Hole

For each selling situation, match the client or customer with the right salesperson. If your customer profile calls for a touchy-feely Pal as a salesperson, don't send a distant and objective Sage and expect much success. If you're selling to a business, use both company culture and individual contacts as a proxy for the customer profile.

Read between the lines. You'll have to draw your own inferences about some of your customers' needs. Nobody admits wanting a Pit Bull to hound him until he gives in, but many bottom line–oriented customers will be more inclined to buy from a Pit Bull if the price is right. Some customers also like the Pit Bull's all-business approach and find Pals nosy or annoying.

> **Assess your sales force. Once you've identified the type of salesperson you need for each target customer, review your current sales team to see how it stacks up.**

Some situations are simple. I used to call on Hershey Chocolate Company. This is a company whose employees almost never quit. It's very family-oriented, lots of nice people, small-town feel (basically, the company owns the town). To sic a Pit Bull on Hershey would be crazy. This would be a job for a Pal or a Sage.

On the other hand, I also sold to General Mills, which was more competitive, more of a transition company. General Mills was also difficult to bag, so I needed to be both Pit Bull and Pal with that client.

Assess your sales force. Once you've identified the type of salesperson you need for each target customer, review your current sales team to see how it stacks up. If you own a shoe store, for instance, you may have to replace a sophisticated Sage with an unassuming Pal in order to sell gym shoes to kids and teens.

Matching the right salesperson with the right situation benefits not only you, but the salesperson as well. People thrive in a job setting that suits their talents and personality.

Through this process, you might learn that your selling situation requires a type of salesperson you currently lack. If you decide to fill this slot, you can use the information to build a description of your ideal candidate before you list the job. It may be necessary to replace or reshuffle some of your sales force if you can't get what you need any other way.

Efren Hernandez owns Same Day Printing, a small neighborhood quick-print business in Manhattan. Efren sells

The Sales Force's Triple Threat: The Chameleon

A true master salesperson can shift from one personality category to another, depending on the situation. She might be a Pit Bull at a 9:00 AM meeting, a jovial Pal for her 10:30 AM meeting, then a Sage for her 2:00 PM meeting.

When I learned how to be a Chameleon, I found that this broke the day up nicely for me and made it more interesting. I'd begin by quickly assessing the person I was trying to sell. Typically, if the contact was younger than me or was given my name on a referral, I'd end up selling as a Sage, communicating the details of the product and reinforcing my knowledge. As the Sage, my underlying message was "You can trust me—you're young and inexperienced, and I'll show you the way."

Often, if I was selling to a resource department (see chapter 13), I'd be a Pal. The folks in this line of work are more interested in enjoying their working relationships than most workers. I'd usually entertain these people a bit more as well.

Sometimes a potential customer was so wishy-washy that he was almost begging to be forced into a decision. In this case, my Pit Bull persona would pay a visit. The Pit Bull was also necessary when I sold to a more competitive Elephant or in a competitive marketplace.

Learn to be a Chameleon by not having preconceived notions about the customer. Remember that Elephants are people, too. If a company is heavy in bureaucracy, this doesn't necessarily mean that all its personnel are high-strung and uptight, or that if a company is based in New York, you have to be a Pit Bull. Take the time to assess—then proceed as necessary.

to individuals who walk into the store, and his two salespeople, Keith and Alex, are responsible for selling to small business accounts.

Efren was concerned that although Alex was bringing in five or ten new customers every week, Keith was struggling to get one new account a month. Efren couldn't understand why. After all, Keith had far more experience than Alex and knew the printing business cold. It wasn't as if Keith were lazy; Efren had been monitoring Keith's activity and was convinced he was trying hard, even if to no avail.

I encouraged Efren to compare his two salesmen's personalities. Then I told him to profile the small businesses that were their sales targets. Finally, I suggested that he stand beside Keith and watch him at work.

Efren called me a week later and told me what he had observed. Together, we determined that Keith, the printing expert, was the proverbial Sage. Alex, on the other hand, knew little about printing but was adept at cultivating relationships with customers—the classic Pal.

Efren had also called many of his clients and local businesses to ask them how they chose their quick printers. Although Efren's customers wanted quality printing at a fair price, what really mattered to them was whom they worked with, day to day. In that contest, Alex was primed to win from the outset.

This isn't to say that printers should always hire Pals as salespeople. In a different business environment—say, a large-volume, high-ticket print industry, where experience and quality are the sole reasons for selecting a printer—Keith, the Sage, would be the ideal salesman.

Now came the hard part: what to do? Although Efren could have let Keith go, he decided to capitalize on Keith's experience by bumping him up to sales manager, where he could facilitate the closing process by contributing the experience that Alex lacked. Efren also hired another Pal to fill Keith's old position.

I recently heard from Efren. Everyone at Same Day Printing was happy, including Keith, who was glad to be working in a role that suited him. Today Efren has five Pals selling for him, and his business is booming.

Matchmaking

Here's a great example of how important it is to have an effective front person when you're making contacts inside the big company. I had been trying for two years to land a contract with a huge packaged-goods company in the Bay Area. I was getting some business but couldn't seem to score that home run. I tried and tried to develop a relationship with a key manager, but had no luck. This bothered me; I had always considered relationships to be one of my strong suits.

Apparently I was wrong in this case. The guy was uptight and unresponsive, to say the least.

Most of the company's business traveled across this candidate's desk, and even though he didn't have a specific budget, almost all marketing spending went through him. I was certain that this guy was the best candidate to be our champion at the company. Our services were good, so if he were on our side, we'd score big-time business. But since I wasn't having any luck with him, I didn't think I was the person to approach him. That called for someone with a more low-key, sensitive demeanor. I decided to fire myself and assign a different salesperson.

The person I chose, Denise, was a consummate Pal—sincere, friendly, smart, and professional, the best I'd ever seen at developing champions, a natural at the game. I told her it would be a challenge. As always, she was up for it—but secretly, I must confess, I thought it was an impossible task.

I was at home on a Thursday night when Denise phoned to let me know (and to rub it in my face a bit) that she had just returned from having dinner with the hard-nosed customer and his wife, at their house!

After she convinced me she wasn't pulling my leg, I went into a blissed-out sort of shock. We went on to sell this customer more than $3 million in services over the next few years. This proved to me that anyone could be converted into a champion under the right circumstances, and although I didn't manage to click with him, my salesperson succeeded—and was rewarded big time with hefty commissions.

Face-to-Face with Your Prospect

Preparing Yourself and Your Pitch

If your telephone and mail efforts have hit paydirt, you're about to go face-to-face with a potential client. Just as in any other aspect of life, first impressions are crucial. You want to come across as perceptive, experienced, and confident—a professional who works with big companies every day. The following tips will help pave your way.

Get Your Act Together

Don't prepare a one-size-fits-all sales spiel that can be rattled off in any meeting. To the extent possible, go into the meeting with a discussion plan tailored to that particular Elephant. Your earlier contacts with the prospect should have given you the information you need. If not, go back to your reconnaisance of the company. Be ready to discuss whatever you specified during the meeting setup call. In addition:

Set priorities. Before every important meeting, I make a list of specifics I hope to accomplish. This helps me stay focused; when I'm face-to-face with my prospect, I sneak an occasional peek to make sure all my issues have been addressed. Having a written list helps me avoid getting distracted by issues the prospect raises. These have to be addressed, of course, but not at the risk of forgetting the things that can make the difference between a good deal for the prospect and a good deal for me. Once I've achieved my top priorities, I go for more.

Anticipate your prospect's concerns. What questions is he likely to ask? Be ready to provide answers. Better yet, prepare documents that can help answer these questions, as well as others that can clarify your answers: sell sheets, product specifications, process explanations, and so forth.

One question a lot of my prospects used to ask when considering using one of my companies was "How will I know that the people I specify are actually receiving the marketing materials?" Rather than giving them vague reassurances, I always came prepared for this question by drawing up a detailed flow chart outlining the procedures my company followed to make sure it happened. I also brought our documents to life by providing videotape of deliveries we had made using these procedures. This worked well; not only did the materials give legitimacy to my words, they also provided the contact something to pass on to his bosses, the real decision makers.

> **Never give a prospect reason to think that you are not taking the meeting seriously.**

Prepare. Above all, never give a prospect reason to think that you are not taking the meeting seriously. If you haven't gathered all the information you were supposed to have obtained in your first phone contact (see chapter 7, "Step 3: Phone Call #1"), it's perfectly acceptable to contact the prospect before the meeting with any questions on the products or services you're going to discuss. Preface your call by saying that, because you value his time, you want to learn about your prospect's needs so that you can focus on what's most important to him during the meeting.

In the Arena

Why is it important to be prepared before you walk onto the playing field for your first meeting with the prospect? Because your self-assurance is a major factor in how well you will do in the negotiation, and preparation is the key. With the assurance of knowing the answers to the most likely questions, you can approach every negotiation with the attitude that you're the experienced professional, the master of your game, the essential ingredient in the big company's success. (But don't let your self-confidence grow into arrogance; you bluff the Elephant at your peril.)

Focus on the prospect. Don't make the common mistake of talking too much about yourself or your business. Your time is limited—usually less than one hour in which to win over your prospect and get to the next level. Don't waste it all on matters of no importance to your audience.

As you walk to the meeting room with your prospect, use the time wisely. Establish rapport by using a pleasant conversational tone; tell an amusing story. Once the meeting starts, here's a good way to proceed: before explaining what your business does and how you can help, get your prospect to tell you something about her own business and its needs. The more you can get her to talk, the faster you'll figure out the best way to sell to her. Then you can tailor your material and use your time more effectively.

If your prospect is serious, she'll ultimately be using information from your proposal in her own internal analysis. If you can give her a proposal or quote in a format that's easy for her, you're miles ahead of the game.

Team up. Your odds are better if two or more of your people are at the meeting. In fact, you can greatly increase your advantage if you and the others know how to play a team game.

One way to leverage your person power is to use a variation of the legendary "good cop, bad cop" ploy. I would sometimes play the seasoned pro and bring along a younger sales rep as a wet-behind-the-ears tyro. The "kid" would ask a lot of naive questions and be answered with patient explanations. Later, I would explain to the prospect privately that my associate was new to the industry and I was helping him learn the business. Not only did this make me look like a good guy, we obtained a lot of useful information—things an experienced sales rep might not know but might be reluctant to ask.

On the other hand, teams must be careful not to monopolize the discussion. When I took others to a meeting, we had an understanding that no one was to interrupt or shout down the prospect in the heat of negotiation. We also used a code: if one of us started talking too much, another would scratch his nose as a cautionary signal. You'd be amazed at how quickly I could shut up when informed by a team member that I was off base.

Follow their format. Remember what I said about bureaucracy? Imagine having to conform to a detailed internal analysis sheet and needing to extract pieces of information from a confusing proposal. This is tedious at best; at worst, it simply won't happen, and you're out of luck. Now put this same person in front of a proposal that clearly outlines the information pertinent to her internal document. I'm sure you see the advantage.

> **Once you know the format and information needed, make sure to submit every quote and proposal in that style.**

Once you know the format and information needed, make sure to submit every quote and proposal in that style. I've asked prospects for a copy of their company's internal analysis document, explaining that I want to make their life easier. First, however, find out what your prospect's company calls this form. This makes you sound knowledgeable about her company and makes it easier for her to say yes to your request. Most prospects will say no, citing internal confidentiality—but all you need is for one person to say yes, then you're all set for the rest.

If you can't get a copy of this document, make sure to ask specifically what information she requires, and whether she prefers a short summary or a long, detailed proposal. Because she's busy, she'll actually appreciate your doing much of the work. Once you have her input, be sure to follow her suggestions. She might tell you to keep your proposal to one page and avoid any hype; she might want you to lay out the benefits of your product; or she might want something else entirely.

After the Meeting

The game doesn't end when the meeting is over. In fact, it's just beginning. The only sure sign of success is the prospect's signature on the bottom line.

Follow through. If you've stirred your prospect's interest, you'll come out of meetings with questions or requests to address. Don't fall into the common trap of forgetting to respond because you have too many other meetings to attend or phone calls to make. Take a minute after each meeting to write up a quick recap and to-do list. Then get whatever information your prospect needs right away. If you're having trouble responding quickly to a request, let the prospect know you're working on answers to his questions. He'll take your response speed and accuracy as a prime indicator of your quality of delivery.

Seal the deal. All this goodwill and advice isn't worth much if you haven't closed the deal. We'll discuss negotiating strategies a bit later, but for now, don't be afraid to ask for what you need. Establish timelines and stick to them. At the same time, avoid such transparent tactics as the "impending doom" close—claiming that after such-and-such date, your service won't be available or the price will go up. Hackneyed techniques like this usually backfire and can make you look amateurish; most Elephants can see right through them. That said, you can and should apply whatever legitimate pressure you can muster. Ideally you'll find yourself in a favorable situation—perhaps finding one of the Elephant's competitors who wants to buy your service—that can provide leverage to encourage your prospects to close.

A Few More Tips

Here are several more pointers that can help you get the ink on the dotted line:

Get your prospect vested. The more time and energy

your client has invested in your getting the order, the better; after all, she doesn't like seeing her efforts come to naught any more than you do. Involve her, but don't harp. When you call, make it a good reason, one that's relevant to the project.

Simplify the prospect's life. Often your prospect will need to plug your numbers into a payout model, compare your services to the competition, or even reformat your proposal into a style desired by his management. I once had a client who had to take all the information from all the suppliers and aggregate it into one-page overviews. These overviews included such topics as strategic rationale (why the prospect should use them), cost, and payout.

Burnish your credibility. When you first start to get business, perhaps the most difficult hurdle is trust. Your prospects have careers to worry about, so they might be reluctant to try new suppliers. Seek to boost your credibility in any way possible. Send examples of your work, especially if it's for other large companies, or send articles about your business—anything to eliminate the perceived risk of doing business with the new guy.

Cultivate relationships. People generally like to help other people, especially when it's someone they like. Don't be afraid to ask for help when you need it. This includes asking who does what, when the budget season starts, what's the correct proposal format, how results are evaluated—even where your price should be in order to be competitive. You'll be surprised at what you hear.

Introduce the family. As you spend more time with your Elephant, bring some of your operations people along to visit with people they know only by phone. This will help them feel they're a valued part of the organization. It will also give them better understanding of the company's situation and motivate them to respond to your requests.

Who makes the call? Make sure you know who influences, who buys, and who kills (see chapter 4). Ask your prospect if there are any other issues or concerns you should address.

Make it personal. Ask for the order. Don't sound desperate, but convey a commitment to doing a great job for your prospect. Make it known that you'll baby-sit the project to ensure its success. By so doing, you also forge a tighter relationship with your prospect, who now feels that he has gone to bat for you. Then make sure that the project comes off great.

Manage the intensity. Come across as professional and dedicated, but not fanatical. Balance the desire for the sale with the need to enjoy what you're doing. If the prospect says she'll have an answer for you on Wednesday, don't call on Monday and Tuesday to see if she's made a decision—you'll just seem desperate. Wait until Wednesday, then call to see if she needs any more information.

Learn from no. If you don't get the business, ask why. Make sure the prospect doesn't feel any need to spare your feelings; let him know that he'll be helping you by telling you the real reason, no matter how harsh. Don't get defensive, argue with him, or try to explain. You can ask specific questions to get more info; for example, if he says he wasn't sure you could deliver on time, ask what gave him that impression. Thank him for his input, learn from it, and go get the next one.

Standing Up to Your Elephant

Negotiating from Your Strengths

Sprawling campuses, tall buildings, smartly dressed executives, deep pockets—large corporations are impressive, right? And a bit intimidating, too, when you think that the key to your own fabulous wealth is hidden somewhere nearby. All that money and power! What must it be like to be part of such a magnificent company!

Well, as you've often heard, the grass is always greener. Many's the middle manager who would leave his giant company in a minute to have the freedom you enjoy. Even well-paid executives get tired of the bureaucracy; they long to be their own boss, make their own decisions, live or die by their wits—just like you, you renegade.

But at least a person's salary and career security are better in the big company, right? Well, actually, you stand a good chance of making more money than most of the corporate types you deal with. And security? Talk to some of the laid-off corporate employees who call me looking for work.

No, the main advantage people in large corporations have is the deep pockets backing them up. When they're negotiating with a smaller company like yours, they've got the upper hand: You want our big money? You do things our way, see?

Or so it might seem.

Negotiating with Your Elephant

Sometimes large companies do use their enormous financial power as a bargaining tool. They may say, "Give us a rock-bottom price, and you'll make it up in volume." What they don't have to say is, "If you're going to be hard-nosed, we can always sign a lucrative contract with your competitor."

Nevertheless, whether your counterpart across the table is a low-level employee or a senior vice president, you can neutralize much of that leverage if you follow a few key guidelines when negotiating with an Elephant.

Negotiate with a person, not a company. How often have you heard, "I'd love to say yes, but my boss won't let me," or "I think it's a good deal, but company policy prohibits me from saying yes"? That's the weight of a huge company bearing down on you. Ignore it. You're not talking to a faceless entity who has no choice but to play hardball, as he would like you to believe; you're talking to a person, and that person has the power to make choices and decisions. Negotiate accordingly.

> **You're talking to a person, and that person has the power to make choices and decisions. Negotiate accordingly.**

Remember, however, that your opposite number is probably being evaluated on his performance, and that performance includes not only getting the lowest price but also vendor reliability, quality of service, and other factors. Don't buckle on the important points, but build into your offer a few terms you can yield on to let the other guy save face. (See the next topic.)

Prioritize your gives. Decide beforehand what really matters and what doesn't—and which points you can concede in order to appear magnanimous. If you find yourself at the end of your price-cutting tether, look for throw-ins you can add to the deal to make the client feel the company is getting more value for its money. But be sure to check for added cost.

What's important to the customer? Your prospect may be negotiating for a price cut for any of a number of reasons, including (a) to comply with a recent budget cut, (b) to lower the price of her own product or service, or (c) simply to impress her boss with how tough a negotiator she is. Try to figure out her motives; your intuition may play a big role here. For example, you may be able to lower the price as a favor to help her meet budget goals—in return for the guarantee of another contract down the line.

Don't surrender too quickly. Your prospect will smell blood and he'll only want more. Rather than agreeing to all points up front—even when you've already decided to accept his terms—tell your prospect that you'll have to get back to him after you check with your management. This will give the impression that he's doing a good job and that you're working to get your management to give in.

Give yourself cover. If you're in sales, you have the cover of your senior management. But if you own your own business and also sell to clients, it's sometimes wise not to mention that you own the business. If the client knows you're the owner, she may try to make you feel you must give in or risk damaging your relationship with her. If she doesn't know, you can let her down easy and blame it on your nameless, faceless senior management—the same tactic Elephants use on you.

Though I never lied about it, very few of my clients knew that I was the owner of my company. This strategy also made it easier for some of the lower-level employees I was dealing with to relate to me as a working stiff, just like them.

If you own the business but employ others to sell to your clients, you may have to play the bad guy to protect your salesperson's relationship with the client. However, you may be able to shift the blame (and remain the good guy) by telling the client you have to discuss the negotiated point with your partners.

Don't sell yourself short. The prospect is at the negotiating table for a reason. If you didn't offer some promise of benefit to the company, he wouldn't waste his time talking with you.

Mitigate all pricing concessions. Remember that once you lower your price, you'll almost never be able to raise it again. If you must do so anyway, have the company "give a give"—commit in writing to a volume buy or reduced service levels so you can still make a profit. Make sure to note the difference between your normal price for goods or services and the reduced price you charged. Send a copy to the customer, and keep this explanation handy so that when the next deal comes up and your customer expects the reduced pricing again, you can pull out your sheet and let him know that the price paid last time didn't include all services, product features, or other factors. And hold firm—it's probably your only chance to reposition your pricing back where it should be.

In general, look for a long-term deal in exchange for a lower price. That way, you'll have more time to profit from the increased volume; you'll enjoy continued access to the client; and you'll go to sleep that night knowing that you have revenue and commissions booked for years into the future.

Reverse Internet Auction

Big companies are beginning to exploit the new, online marketplace more and more often to drive prices down in a "reverse auction." Here's how it works.

- Suppliers fill out proposals for a project, giving the customer information about what's important in the project—their qualifications, prices, delivery, new ideas, etc.

- Several companies are selected, given passwords, and invited to participate in a reverse auction.

- In this online bidding frenzy, competitors bid live against each other for the project. Each supplier can see the prices going down, down, down; they just don't know which companies are undercutting them.

- Because they bid on a line-item basis, competitors usually end up with only a portion of the project.

Should you find yourself in this situation, just follow the strategies outlined on these pages. Don't bid yourself out of any chance of making a profit.

Bid resolutely. One of the ways Elephants ferret out the lowest price is to turn your product or service into a commodity—something that's easily supplied by others and priced at the mercy of supply and demand. They do this by putting the project out for bid.

Of course, when you're pitching them, that's what they're doing, anyway—meeting everyone, assessing which of you they like and who can do the job, then trying to get the lowest price. The difference with bids is that the customer is being up front by asking suppliers to go head to head in a price battle. It's a tough, uncomfortable situation, but there are ways to handle it.

Create a pricing strategy and stick to it. Whether it's based on margins or cost-plus, decide on a price that's fair and reasonable for everyone, then stick to that price when negotiating. If the project is put up for bid after you've disclosed your price, it shouldn't really matter, because you shouldn't come off your price that much anyway. Either you'll get the business or you won't. If you commoditize your offerings, it'll be tough to get your full price ever again. And if your project is up for rebid, keep in mind that you stand a pretty good chance of winning the bid, but probably after negotiating yourself out of 10 percent or more of your profit.

Don't sacrifice quality for the deal. If you keep reducing price, you'll eventually get to the point where you're losing money or at most breaking even. At this point, you'll be tempted to cut back on quality. The result? Your chances for future business go out the window, and your reputation gets besmirched. Sometimes it's better to take a pass and let the other guy bomb.

> **Remember, it's not always the lowest bidder who gets the contract.**

Make it clear how you are different from the other bidders, and better. If you feel, for example, that you'll need to include additional processes in order to provide the quality controls the big company is asking for, mention that in your proposal, along with the extra cost. Remember, it's not always the lowest bidder who gets the contract.

Handle RFPs with care. Some companies routinely issue an RFP (request for proposal) to standardize the bidding process for an item or service. It's a double-edged sword. If you get a contract by responding to an RFP, it will probably be large—but there's usually only one winner, and if it's you and you haven't been careful about pricing for profit, your bid can lock you into a low profit margin for a long time. The company gets a good look at how you plan to handle specific issues, leaving you little flexibility. It can also see how much fat is in other contracts you may have with it.

My Kingdom for a Champion . . .

Although I've had some luck dealing with RFPs, the RFP that stands out in my mind is one of the biggest I've ever tackled.

Burger King had put out an RFP for a huge global marketing contract that included advertising, market research, technology, and much more—a bonanza for any marketing firm, large or small.

The RFP involved multiple steps and a lot of out-of-pocket expenses. First, you submitted a top-line document so Burger King could weed out financially weak businesses. Second, if you were selected, you had to complete a detailed RFP. If you made it over this hurdle, you had to conduct a two-hour presentation, then answer questions about your plan.

Our detailed RFP cost me several weeks of full-time work by more than twenty of my people, including my senior personnel. We videotaped customers at Burger King, created a detailed, Internet-based program management and communication function, and included a complete global customer service infrastructure. Our proposal was a four-inch-thick book with a CD-ROM.

By the time we were selected as one of three finalists, our costs had become astronomical—and I was still looking at flying ten people to Florida from various parts of the world for a one-day presentation. Nevertheless, we went for it. Our presentation went great, and we got a lot of positive feedback.

We went home. The days ticked by. I called and called but wasn't able to try the usual sales magic on this Elephant because I didn't know anyone inside Burger King. I had no champions, no alliances.

Ten days later, we got our answer: Thanks, but we're going with someone else.

It was a bummer—spending so much, coming so close, then losing—but I learned a harsh lesson. Never go in blind. If you don't have access to information about the Elephant's true priorities, it's probably better to walk away and go looking for simpler, less expensive RFPs.

Big companies sometimes use the RFP to reduce your sophisticated strategy to a collection of line-item commodities. They might ask you to break out costs for creative, design, production, freight, and other activities—or even indicate how much you're making on the project. Resist this as best you can. I've walked away from an RFP rather than itemize my company costs, because once the big customer understands these, you'll be fighting an uphill battle on every contract that follows. It's better to walk away from one contract than to get hammered on many.

> **Don't let your ego or the urge to win at all costs take over your thinking. It's better to walk away from one contract than to get hammered on many.**

Don't let your ego or the urge to win at all costs take over your thinking. I've seen many companies become history because they were so determined to win an RFP that they gave away the store to do it. Bidding an RFP is an art. If you intend to play in the RFP arena, I strongly urge you to find a consultant or hire a full-time expert. If you don't know how to do it, it'll be a tough road.

Count services as costs. As you seek contracts with bigger companies, you might find that your business needs to hire more personnel, add processes to increase quality control, or provide services you don't normally offer to smaller businesses. Most of these cost money. Be sure to account for them in your costs before you promise them to the client.

Several years ago, I was helping Sam Dion get his business, Big D Printing, on the right track. Big D Printing was a local print house specializing in medium-size printing runs. Sam's business was just chugging along, year after year, neither growing much nor making a lot of money.

In an effort to make his business take off, Sam made the commitment to go after the big customer. He focused on several companies that met his criteria, and after eight months of hard work he bagged his first Elephant, a huge manufacturing company in his hometown. Sam was beaming, and rightfully so. The competition for printing business is fierce, and bagging his Elephant was no easy task.

Once the customer agreed to give Big D some work, it came time to negotiate the contract. Sam was stuck in the "please the client" mode—a dangerous place to be when negotiating a contract. Whatever the customer asked for, even items not included in the quote, Sam said, "No problem." To ensure printing quality, the customer wanted press checks: "No problem." They wanted cartons of finished pieces to weigh no more than twenty pounds, rather than Big D's customary forty pounds: "No problem." They wanted the printed pieces shrink-wrapped in bundles of 250: "No problem." And sent to four different locations. "No problem."

> **Often it doesn't even occur to the customer that his requests are costing you money, and if you don't pass along the added costs, why should he offer to pay them?**

You can see where this is going, can't you? Pretty soon, Sam was working for free. He was so befuddled by his big win that he let down his guard and gave back all the profits. Sad, because he could have avoided it by following the above advice. Big companies can often pull money from other funds to pay for delivery and other costs. They probably would have given in on the costly packaging, anyway. Either way, Big D wouldn't have shouldered the extra cost and the margin hit that came with it.

Of course, you don't want to be difficult. You want to be a good partner. But remember—a partnership works both ways. Often it doesn't even occur to the customer that his requests are costing you money, and if you don't pass along the added costs to him, why should he offer to pay them? Your client, who has probably never owned a business himself, figures that if you aren't saying anything, his requests are at most a minor inconvenience.

Tell him what the extras will cost. Then let him decide. And if you do want to give him a freebie, make sure he knows the specific hit to profits your nice gesture has meant.

Boost margins with add-ons. In dealing with big companies over many years, I've found that once you get going with these guys there's huge upside money coming your way through requests, changes, and other add-ons—if you're tuned in to it. A developer building a home charges for alterations or upgrades you request to the plan or materials.

You should work the same way. Changes in your processes, alterations to the product or service you quoted, increased manpower, quality control, or anything else your Elephant asks for that costs you money (as was the case with Big D Printing), you're clearly entitled to charge a fee and make a profit or commission on it.

Now, I'm not saying that you should be looking for ways to gouge your Elephant—be careful, because Elephants aren't fond of being gouged—but it will be asking for many things, and you shouldn't be afraid to charge for them. In my businesses I would anticipate 3 to 5 percent additional fees off the contracted amount at higher profit margin simply for these add-ons. Chapters 13 and 14 discuss more strategies to maximize your income from your big customers.

Recruiting Great Champions

Courting and Cultivating Your Inside Sales Rep

As you begin to meet with your prospect and your relationship grows, you will need to establish your credibility and gain access to the levers of power. For those tasks, you need a champion.

A champion is an individual in the prospective company who goes to bat for you by trying to get her company to use your services. A strong champion can shorten your ramp-up time with the client and do wonders for your company image. She speaks on your behalf during closed-door meetings and passes your name around to her co-workers.

Simply by interacting with different people, you'll usually gravitate toward the champion who's meant for you. Everyone's a potential champion—and you'll need as many as you can get. Once you mesh with a potential champion, work to make her your own. Help her be successful by giving great service and quality. As you learn more about what she views as important work, come through for her. I had one champion who merely wanted to know how everyone else in the company was reacting to her marketing ideas. I was a great source of information for her, and she made sure I kept getting business by supporting me in the company.

My first champion at Procter & Gamble was Daryl, an assistant marketing brand manager who worked on the Pert brand. Daryl wanted to try one of our programs, but there was a problem—we weren't an "authorized core vendor," a term I had never even heard of. Daryl took it upon himself to make sure we understood everything we needed to do in order to become an authorized supplier. He went out on a limb for our small, unknown company, and I've never forgotten it to this day. As the years went by, we added many new champions, across many departments, to the fold.

> **A strong champion can shorten your ramp-up time with the client and do wonders for your company image.**

Anatomy of a Great Champion

As you spend more time communicating with your prospect, keep your eyes open for a champion, bearing in mind that your best champion is:

Motivated by what's best for the business. She makes decisions based on what's good for her employer, not on politics. This is the easiest champion to win over, because you can appeal to her on a quality-of-service basis. Your work ethic and results will make the difference in her business.

Respected by his superiors. Management looks to him for solid business recommendations. This can come in the form of written recommendations, but mostly it happens when he is approached in the hallway and asked for advice on a matter or a specific supplier. You need to be on his short list of recommended suppliers. If you're on the outs with him, you can forget about getting much business, because he has lots of clout.

Socially networked. People like a champion, so his endorsement carries added weight and cachet. You'll hear

Build a Prospect Organization Chart

As you begin to call around and learn more about how the company operates, figure out who reports to whom and where everyone fits. If you can't get an organization chart from your champion, ask questions such as "Who else will be involved in the decision?" or "Is there anyone else with whom you'd like me to discuss this?" On these two pages are examples of the organization charts that we developed as we tried to break into P&G and when Touching Memories Custom Stationery was gaining business at one of its larger prospects. The page opposite shows an example of what a typical Elephant organizational structure might look like. Procter & Gamble has recently changed its structure to address the global needs of consumers, but this example still serves.

Touching Memories Custom Stationery

Human Relations Department

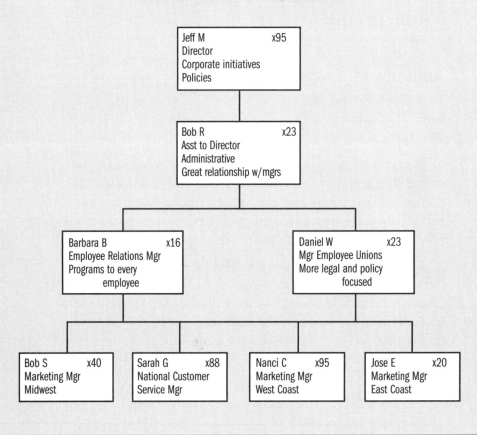

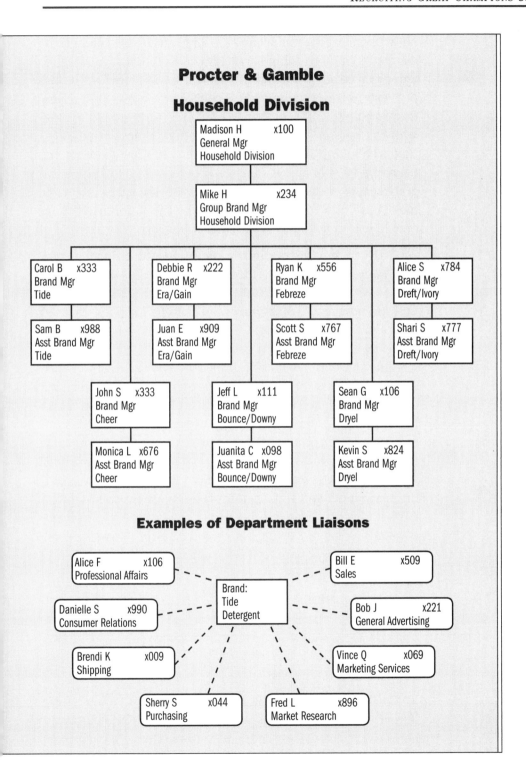

Procter & Gamble
Household Division

Madison H   x100
General Mgr
Household Division

Mike H   x234
Group Brand Mgr
Household Division

Carol B   x333
Brand Mgr
Tide

Debbie R   x222
Brand Mgr
Era/Gain

Ryan K   x556
Brand Mgr
Febreze

Alice S   x784
Brand Mgr
Dreft/Ivory

Sam B   x988
Asst Brand Mgr
Tide

Juan E   x909
Asst Brand Mgr
Era/Gain

Scott S   x767
Asst Brand Mgr
Febreze

Shari S   x777
Asst Brand Mgr
Dreft/Ivory

John S   x333
Brand Mgr
Cheer

Jeff L   x111
Brand Mgr
Bounce/Downy

Sean G   x106
Brand Mgr
Dryel

Monica L   x676
Asst Brand Mgr
Cheer

Juanita C   x098
Asst Brand Mgr
Bounce/Downy

Kevin S   x824
Asst Brand Mgr
Dryel

Examples of Department Liaisons

Alice F   x106
Professional Affairs

Bill E   x509
Sales

Danielle S   x990
Consumer Relations

Brand:
Tide
Detergent

Bob J   x221
General Advertising

Brendi K   x009
Shipping

Vince Q   x069
Marketing Services

Sherry S   x044
Purchasing

Fred L   x896
Market Research

co-workers asking him what he's doing after work, and other clients talking favorably about him as well. I always made it a point to be seen walking the halls or having lunch with one of these networking wizards. I can't count how many times during lunch someone would come over to the table to talk with the person I was with and mention, almost in passing, that I should stop by later in the day. At that meeting I'd usually get a shot at some business, or at least an invitation to grab a drink or two after work—either of which was fine with me! These little things are what make the difference. They enable you to maximize your success in closing deals.

Able to navigate the company to get things done. She knows how to sell ideas internally. She also knows what not to do and which departments are ineffective. Just imagine how much time you could save by knowing exactly where to focus your efforts. A good champion can tell you, or at least point you in the right direction.

Your champion can be your best asset when dealing with an RFP (request for proposal). She can tell you which parts of the RFP are being given the most weight and which are less important. Once, when I was dealing with an RFP from an electronics company, I learned from my champion that this Elephant was more concerned about having its product arriving in good condition than about cost. I focused my bid on this factor, even adding new protective measures at extra cost—and profit. We won that contract because we gave the company confidence that its product would arrive safely—and because my champion had told me where to focus my attention.

Cut from the same cloth as you. You have chemistry because you share the same business philosophy, work ethic, or background. You enjoy seeing each other and doing business together. You can relate to each other without having to put up a front.

Willing to give credit rather than protect her turf. If your champion isn't actively promoting you and your business, she isn't a true champion. You must have a champion who's willing to share some of the limelight. She must feel that your success and the success of the deal reflect well upon her.

Your Champion in Operation

Once you've set some meetings, called directly on prospects, identified your champions, and begun to develop your business relationships with key people in the company, you're on your way. Stick with the process until you start to get orders. The first several orders may even be disappointingly small. Regard them as opportunities to overperform and give the client time to feel comfortable with you as a supplier. Nothing is more important than doing a great job, for that's the ticket to bigger orders.

It's wise to think of your champion as your inside sales rep. With that in mind, work to give your champion the answers to any possible objections her company might have to your doing business there—features and benefits of your product or service, success stories from other clients, and so forth. Create a one-page "cheat sheet" outlining these points for your champion—and laminate it, so it's less likely to be thrown away.

> **Keep close track of your champion's moves. When he goes to another big company, you've got an automatic inside contact there.**

One final note. In today's business world, capable and popular executives change companies as often as CEOs used to change their socks. Keep close track of your champion's moves. When she goes to another big company, you've got an automatic inside contact there. Use it.

Part IV

LEVERAGING YOUR ELEPHANT'S POWER

Keeping Your Champions Cheering

Treating Your Friends Right

It's a great thing to develop a relationship to the point where you actually have solid champions working your cause from the inside. However, once you've accomplished this task, your job isn't finished. You'll need to foster these relationships over time to keep getting the most out of them.

Here are a few methods I've used to keep my champions willing to go into battle for me:

Share the limelight. Keep in mind that what you're after is business, not attention or accolades. If you share credit with your champions, you'll acquire a reputation as someone easy to work with, and useful. You may even help them get promoted, which means great career news for them—and perhaps more business for you.

During my sales presentations, I often handed out a list of successful projects and the contacts I'd worked with inside the company. The fact that I was generously sharing the credit did not go unnoticed among my prospects. Nor was I oblivious to the fact that these people were known to many of my prospects and, when contacted, would serve as excellent references for my business.

Share the knowledge. Let your champions in on your latest plans. They'll be more comfortable if they know you're working with them, not around them. I maintained a running list of potential projects I was pitching at a company. This kept them informed as to what was new, who was being innovative, and where the biggest promotions were being handed out. This information, along with the juiciest gossip, was useful in building relationships with my champions. It helped me close a lot of deals.

Know when to back off. It's fine to ask your champions to make a call on your behalf, but don't get greedy. You never know when you might really need them, and you don't want them to feel you're exploiting their generosity.

Over my twenty-plus years in business, I can remember very few times when I asked someone for a direct favor. I just wasn't comfortable doing so, and when I did, it was usually to clear up a misunderstanding or to help another champion.

> **You can never have too many champions, and you need them at all levels.**

Make a happy family. Look for new champions as you move up the company ladder. You can never have too many, and you need them at all levels. You never really know who knows whom and who influences whom after working hours.

After several years of calling on your Elephant, you should know at least as many people as a new hire who's been there for six months. I used to smile when I'd meet a brand-new marketing person; I loved being able to give him the inside scoop on his company's terminology and how things got done. Feeling reassured that he was in safe hands among "old pros," he'd help us round up new business.

One Sweet Idea

Keeping my champions happy was a major priority and a continuing activity for me, so important that I'd hold champion development workshops for the businesses I owned or consulted for. In these workshops (which one participant dubbed the "Fun Elephant Focus Group"), salespeople, customer representatives, and others involved in getting big customers discussed creative ways to enhance relationships with champions.

One of the most creative ideas I've ever seen came from one of my own salespeople. We were looking for something light and fun for the customers, something that would be a diversion from their boring, day-to-day corporate activities. The salesman was married to a woman who owned a specialty foods business that made awesome gourmet taffy apples, pretzels, and shortbread. This stuff, which was beyond addictive, was sold via direct mail and through high-end retail stores such as Neiman Marcus.

We couldn't just hand out the goods to big companies as thank yous—most of them had "no gift" policies. So we paid the salesman's wife to put together some sampler boxes. Over the next several weeks, whenever an opportunity arose, we asked our champions to do us a favor: help this woman conduct a market test by sampling her products and telling us which they liked best.

Did it work? You'd better believe it! We got more mileage out of this than anything else we'd ever done. The word spread like wildfire. People were stopping me in the halls of P&G, Kraft, Nestlé, and Warner Lambert, asking if we needed any more participants in our focus group. The positive word of mouth made it easier for us to schedule meetings with people who hadn't even received a sampler—people I had sought to meet for months or years. It's important to note here that we didn't simply pass these out to everyone, as we might have with an update mailing or a holiday observance. We wanted to give our champions something special, and the cachet of being one of the lucky ones certainly did the trick.

Remember your roots. No matter how your business booms, never forget who supported you in the early days. As I began working with big-company clients, I'd start with lower-level contacts as champions; by the time I left, I had champions in high executive positions both here and abroad. I never forgot who helped me get there. I made sure I periodically took my early champions to lunch or dinner to catch up on their lives and careers. It's the right thing to do, and you never know who might be promoted next.

Express gratitude. A simple thank you goes a long way. Grab a lunch check or drop off some chocolates once in a while. Take care of your champions, and be there for them if they need anything.

Give them a stake. The best way to get your champions rooting for you and your business is to give them a personal stake in your success—not a financial stake, but an emotional one. Invite them to tour your office or shop and meet your people. Gently persuade them to invest a bit of their own time. Ask your champions for advice, send them materials to review, call with questions, stop by and visit, let them know you'll be a fixture around the place. Be sure to thank them when their counsel pays off—make your success their success—but take care not to be suffocating or intrusive. If you even get an inkling that they are feeling put off by your actions, back way off—immediately.

> **The best way to get your champions rooting for you and your business is to give them a personal stake in your success.**

Help champions say thank you. If you've developed a good, mutually beneficial relationship with your champion, chances are she will look for new ways to use your products or services in her company. There are actions you can take to encourage her to do so.

If you're selling only one or two items, you're probably making it hard for your champion to say thanks by giving you opportunities for more or bigger sales. Expand your thinking. Keep an eye out for new short- and long-term opportunities in her company; develop or adapt products to meet those needs.

Start with your current offerings and "think vertically." If you sell boxes, offer filler or tape. If you sell pizzas to people carrying bottles of water, add bottled water to your menu. If you sell mortgages, offer appraisals as well. A note of caution: be sure your new offering is of high quality, delivered and executed well. Carelessly rushing new products or services to market has tarnished the reputation of more than one good company.

Whatever you sell, seek to add a consultant or advisory component to it. If you sell printing, exude so much knowledge and insight that the Elephant insists on including you in meetings to hear your opinion. Of course, to maintain your credibility, you must be impartial—which means sometimes you might have to say that your company isn't the right one for a project. You probably can't charge for these services, but in this role you'll reap benefits far more valuable than mere money. You'll acquire higher-level contacts, decision makers and influencers you can call when you need help getting approval on a proposal. You'll gain insights into how top managers are thinking and what they are deciding in meetings you can't attend. Your expertise will continue to grow—as will your value to your other champions.

Taking the Inside Track

Building Strong Alliances

L ike most large companies, Procter & Gamble, a customer of mine for years, employs its own security guards. Suppliers sign in at the front desk, put on visitor's badges, and then wait in the lobby until the person they're supposed to meet traipses down and escorts them to the assigned location. Meetings often occur in one of the many sterile conference rooms on the lobby level, a Siberia far from the action.

At first, this was a big problem for us. If the people we were supposed to meet didn't feel like interrupting their workday to come down to the lobby, they would simply blow off the meeting or refuse to schedule one in the first place. Typically, I would schedule eight to ten sales calls a day. If anything went wrong—if I couldn't reach someone on the phone or if anyone was delayed—I would be late for my next appointment and risk losing that meeting as well.

Badges? We Don't Need No Stinkin' Badges

Actually, we did need the stinkin' badges.

One day, as I sat in the P&G lobby waiting for yet another employee to deign to pick me up, I noticed a man wearing a badge—neither an employee's badge nor a visitor's badge, but a special kind—roaming in and out of the secure areas as he pleased. I knew I had to get myself one of those badges.

I walked across the room and struck up a conversation with this privileged man. I casually slipped in a question about the badge, and he explained that because he was working construction on the new floor, he had been given a rare item at P&G, a contractor's badge.

I spent the next month or so trying to figure out ways to get a contractor's badge so I, too, might one day wander freely around the candy store. Finally, it hit me. I needed to persuade the higher-ups to change my status from supplier to contractor, something that would prove to be a serious challenge.

At this point, my company was generating about $200,000 of business with P&G—better than before, but nothing to write home about, because I still wasn't making much profit. I had been developing a program for one of P&G's departments that targeted several brands in several divisions. I immediately changed my proposal to include "ongoing support," which meant I'd have to meet with those brand managers regularly, as a contractor. I hoped that the new badge would be worth its weight in gold—literally—so I reduced the price of the proposal to make it irresistible while still allowing myself a modest profit.

It worked. I got my contractor's badge.

The result was a dream. Meetings were easier to schedule because no one needed to pick me up. The photo-ID contractor's badge enhanced my credibility, which helped with sales. Rare was the day I didn't pick up business just by roaming the halls or sitting in the cafeteria. I'd hear, "Steve, come here when you have a minute," and the next thing I knew, I'd be writing up another deal.

Not surprisingly, my competitors, with whom I'd always had a great relationship, went nuts when they saw me with the access badge. I never rubbed it in their faces—in fact, I made it a habit to take my badge off whenever I saw them or before I went back to the lobby—but I didn't tell them how I got it, either. Why give away the golden goose?

My obsession with getting this badge might sound silly, but over the years, the badge played no small role in our winning more than $30 million in sales that might have passed us by had I still been in the lobby waiting to be picked up.

I chose this example to illustrate a point: once you have a foot in the door, you can and should leverage that opportunity for more business. It's not an easy task, but it's well worth the effort.

Allies of Three Stripes

Once you're booking sales, know your way around the client, and have at least one in-house champion backing you, it's time to up the ante by seeking and forming alliances.

An alliance will result in your getting business from a company's group, division, or department in exchange for things your ally needs: power, information, or a better work experience. The bottom line for you? More sales at higher margins.

In order to develop alliances, you must first identify which of those three needs applies, then develop a plan to fulfill it. A key step in identifying potential alliance partners lies in learning your client's organizational structure.

Alliances bloom when a department, division, or group of people within a company rely on you as part of their team.

Alliances bloom when a department, division, or group of people within a company rely on you as part of their team. Typically, alliances take shape once you've worked with a group for a while and they feel confident that you have their best interests at heart. You add so much value to their team that they treat you as an equal instead of just a contractor or supplier (a term I always hated).

An alliance can be a great catalyst for success. It can expose you to opportunities throughout the client company that you would never be privy to on your own.

Most large companies have many departments, which can be sorted into three categories. The actual category that applies to a given department will vary across companies, but you can place virtually every department in one of these three categories.

Here's how to approach these corporate departments and turn them into allies.

Department Types and Examples

Profit Holders	Necessities	Resources
Brand or service group	Packing	Market research
Product	Sales	Marketing services
	Purchasing	Marketing operations
	Manufacturing	Legal
	Accounting	Research & development
		New business development
		Client services

Profit Holder departments are the keepers of the budget. They monitor income and outflow. They're the most powerful of the departments and thus ultimately responsible for whether the products make a buck. Ask yourself whether this department is responsible for creating the budget rather than simply following it. If so, then the department is a Profit Holder, as is also the case when you hear that your contact is waiting for approval from someone in another department before the company can buy your product. The department controlling the approval would be the profit and loss owner, or Profit Holder.

Because these departments hold the purse strings, they can provide your most rewarding alliances. Remember that they're judged solely on the bottom line. People working for them are on the upper-management track and need to perform. To that end, emphasize your own efficiency and effectiveness at providing the best return on their money.

I once ran a data company that sold names for use in market research. One approach I often used was to get several different Profit Holders in the same company intrigued by the same database list. This way they'd share the costs. Although my company made fewer sales in the end because we had to spread the wealth among more clients, we made much more profit per sale. The increased number of client contacts improved our bottom line and allowed us to expand our customer base at that company.

After a while, client managers at the company began pairing with each other on their own accord in order to share these costs. Word spread across the company. Soon I was hearing about research studies being performed in divisions I never knew existed. My alliance partner received credit for finding my company and sharing our services, and we benefited from more business.

Necessity departments are crucial to the client's core business. Their daily tasks—shipping, purchasing, and manufacturing, to name a few—typically fall on the cost side of the budget, within the limits set by the Profit Holder departments.

The career paths of employees in Necessity departments are determined less by profitability than by how well they keep the client's company running; therefore, they tend to value comfort and working conditions over stellar performance. They will aggressively support you or bash you, based primarily on whether they feel like working with you. You need to make life easier for them; it's as simple as that.

Unlike the Profit Holder types, Necessity employees often have a more adversarial relationship with the higher-ups and may even be unionized. They're usually eager to share their complaints with you, giving you a clearer picture of what to do and what not to do. If, for example, you are providing printing services for your client, contact the shipping department employee who receives your deliveries to see if he has any special instructions or suggestions for you. The next time you're at the company, take the logistics manager out to lunch; chances are you'll be the first to do so and she will appreciate the attention. You may even learn a great deal at lunch about other printing companies or potential clients.

Resource departments support the Profit Holder and Necessity departments. They sometimes operate without a budget and are not essential to the company's core business, though they may be key to its long-term success. Often these departments have to beg, borrow, or steal money to implement their ideas. Examples include market research, customer service, and new business development. If you get a call from someone who says she's upset because you should have met with her, chances are she's in a Resource department.

Employees in Resource departments have unique concerns. Because they are neither directly tied to the profits of the company (as are the Profit Holder departments) nor vital to the client's core business (as are the Necessity departments), they are always vulnerable to cuts and layoffs and must

Be Careful What You Ask For

Marcus Sandstrom was a salesperson at Pollard Recruitment Services, a twenty-five-person headhunting business in Washington, D.C., that specialized in finance and accounting positions. His business had been struggling, but Marcus was making inroads at a large communications company after placing several employees at its headquarters. Although Marcus had several champions at the company, a Resource department known as Client Services took a particular liking to him because he was quick and reliable.

The communications company recently went public through an initial stock offering. Marcus got a call from his Client Services contact, Dave, who told him that the company was going to use some of its shares to acquire many smaller businesses. Furthermore, it would be doing so at breakneck speed, and with each acquisition the department would need one or more additional finance people.

Marcus immediately started calculating what the commissions might be if he were able to bag this Elephant. More than pleased at being tipped off, Marcus asked how he could get in on the action. Dave said that he planned on recommending him to the CFO to fill all those finance positions.

True to his word, Dave set up a meeting with the CFO. The two men clicked and struck a deal. At a slightly reduced rate, Pollard Recruiting would recruit, train, and place the finance employees needed for the new acquisitions. Marcus would be the sales contact at Pollard, and Dave would remain Marcus's contact at the company.

constantly justify their existence, both in the company as a whole and with respect to their fellow Resource departments. Although many Resource departments are filled with talented employees who provide invaluable services to the Profit Holder folks, they are often derided as havens for the lazy and unambitious. Your job, then, is to help them get past the stereotype and show that they are essential to the company's bottom line.

Whenever appropriate, consider inviting Resource employees to client meetings. This will show them you're in the know and looking out for them. If you do invite them, clear it with your contact first before mentioning it; then casually leave a message by voicemail or e-mail. Tell them you thought they could add to the meeting, and leave it at that.

Marcus didn't expect what followed. Over the next two years, the company bought dozens of smaller businesses. The management team was reportedly "insane," working on deals until 3 AM and paging him at all hours of the day or night. He also had to be ready to travel on a moment's notice.

I recently caught up with Marcus, or what was left of him. He filled me in on his past two years, during which he had placed more than forty-five employees in twenty different cities while logging countless miles in the air, almost never sleeping in his own bed. That said, his compensation and Pollard's business had boomed. Marcus was made a full partner; he'd hired five more employees and made almost a million dollars for himself.

Even so, he decided not to renew his contract with the communications company, not just because of the relentless pace, but also because he could use the referral base he had built over the previous two years to sustain the business without all the crazy hours. Wisely, Marcus had also been grooming someone to take over as the lead contact at the communications company.

As for Dave, he had been promoted to a better position within Client Services, which now took on the added responsibility of easing the transition of the newly acquired companies. In true Resource department fashion, the elevation of Client Services, and Dave's role in it, was due in no small part to Dave's ability to demonstrate just how important he and his department were to his entire company.

Putting Your Elephant to Work

Other Ways a Big Customer Can Help You

Aside from making you wealthy, a strong client can do a great deal for you, your business, and your employees. If you're smart, your relationship with your Elephant should be all you need to catapult your business to success. Take a look at the following areas of business that can and should be fully funded by your big customer.

New Business Development

Seek to expand your business into new markets or services—funded by your clients. If you're selling one item, look for the need to buy others, then use your relationship to sell more. You'll be surprised: once these big clients begin to rely on you, and you deliver for them, they'll want to use you in other parts of the business and will help you develop the capacity to do so. Your ability to use your relationship with these clients to identify such opportunities can provide a huge boost to your business.

When I started working at one client company, my business was primarily delivering marketing programs to the child, family, and teen markets. We had considered developing other markets but knew it would be expensive. For every new program, we'd have to sign up venues such as schools, clubs, and doctors' offices to distribute our program to the consumers, then produce all the samples and start selling the service.

Through our alliances with several of this client's departments, we were able to add programs to the college student, immigrant, and ethnic markets, as well as some others. Our client developed and paid for each of these additional programs, which helped us grow our business dramatically. Why so generous? Our client needed to reach these specific target groups with its advertising, and my business offered a proven, cost-effective way to do so.

It's in the Bag!

As I said, my company specialized in target marketing. However, one day, after a meeting in which I tried to sell another marketing program, I was sitting with Randy, one of my P&G brand manager clients, shooting the breeze about nothing in particular. Randy started complaining because he had to deal with a problem that was becoming a major pain for him.

Naturally, I asked a few questions, and he began to tell me his woes. He had bought a bunch of small, pull-string satin cosmetic bags that his department was planning to use to distribute samples of its latest high-end shampoo formula. The problem? The bags were produced in China but were currently stuck in customs in California, and time was running out on the vendor.

I was intrigued. I pressed for more information. Amazingly, there were more than 5 million bags stuck at customs. That's right, 5 million! I might not be the brightest bulb in the chandelier, but I knew one thing—whoever sold that order would be getting one huge commission.

I asked Randy the million-dollar question: "What's the rollout plan for the bags?" The answer: *40 million bags!*—of which we would be distributing plenty through our regular marketing programs. But whoever was supposed to be supplying the bags had left the door wide open for me to seize yet another opportunity.

I asked Randy if he would like for me to use some connections (of course I had none) and look into getting them released from customs. His answer was a resounding Yes! So off I went.

Lacking any experience in importing, I turned to my industry association and placed urgent calls to every importer I could locate. I asked each of them to come to my office, because I had a potentially huge opportunity for them. After meeting with several, I found one that I believed had the clout and knowledge necessary to get the bags released. Thirty-six hours later, the bags had cleared customs and I was Randy's hero. I even picked up the importer's tab for the client—which was actually nothing, because I persuaded the importer to do it at no charge in exchange for the possibility of a huge, 40-million-bag order to follow. I could have charged Randy's company a fee for this, but that seemed short-sighted and piggish. I felt I'd get more mileage and goodwill out of their knowing I'd picked up the fee.

When I reported to Randy that everything was taken care of, and at no charge, he was beyond happy. All I asked in return was a chance to compete for the balance of the order. These bags were about 25 cents each, which meant that I was asking for a $10 million order—light years ahead of what I had ever imagined!

Once Randy assured me that I'd be given a shot, I was off to China. Now, few if any prospects will pay your costs when you're trying to sell to them, and I certainly didn't have the kind of money to afford a trip to China on the chance of winning a contract for bags for client A (Randy). So how did I finance my trip? I was also working with another Procter & Gamble department, client B, that had international responsibilities. These folks were doing the same things in China that I was doing for them in the U.S. However, they loved our controls and security better than what they had in China. I persuaded client B to send me there to review their controls for safeguarding the quality and timeliness of their delivery. I would charge client B only my expenses. Meanwhile, I would go after the really big

> **I could have charged Randy's company a fee for this, but that seemed short-sighted and piggish. I felt I'd get more mileage and goodwill out of their knowing I'd picked up the fee.**

dough—the $10 million bag order for client A.

While working with client B's China office, I asked them to recommend someone they would trust to oversee a business operation. They named Field Force and its amazing and visionary chairman, Steve Chang. So I hired Chang's company to audit my 40-million-bag project for client A. They proposed having their employees sleep at the thirty-plus factories during production to check box counts and material quality, rotating to a different factory every week so the factory managers couldn't buy them off. Steve and I met with several manufacturers and negotiated a great price for the bags. Client A was impressed by my proposal—not to mention my connections.

Bottom line? I had to travel to China four times in four months for P&G client B, but I got the order I was after—40 million bags for P&G client A, manufactured and imported for just over $10 million—and made just over $2 million for my efforts. My client Randy was overjoyed. And I now had another business to offer, one with an impressive résumé, all paid for at a nice profit by my Elephant.

This is a good example of how, with absolutely no experience but with some access and a fire in the belly, you can hit it big time with a single large order. Remember, though, your reputation is on the line. I knew that by asking for the bag order I was, in essence, agreeing to go to a country where I had never been and baby-sit the order. It had to come through, or my core business would be in jeopardy. However, I wasn't worried; I wouldn't have sent a proposal for the order if we couldn't have handled it internally. If I didn't feel comfortable about it, I could have declined the business and still come out ahead: they would have appreciated and respected my decision and gained more confidence in my core business. Once I knew the important factors, it was a no-lose proposition.

Look for opportunities to meet the needs of your customers. Think beyond your core business into complementary pursuits. Then act! Thinking alone won't get it done. If you're handling one aspect of a project, look for ways to vertically integrate the project—own the whole chain of events—so you can get more business.

Training and Expertise

Look for ways to grow and learn from your client's knowledge base. If the client company needs an additional service from you or has a department that performs a service you can integrate with your other services, see if you can get them to train your employees. Tell them that training your staff will help you support them. You may be surprised at their answer.

We needed to build our market research capability for a particular client. Because the company valued working with us, they actually trained our staff (we had fewer than ten employees at the time) and worked with our research person so we could provide them with better service, tailored to their specifications. This line of work turned into a completely independent and immediately profitable endeavor for us, and we started charging other clients for market research.

Many large companies run their own training sessions and bring in national speakers to give presentations to their employees. Some of the best speakers I ever heard were courtesy of a client. Ask if some of your employees working on a company's account can attend. However, make sure your client doesn't perceive you as taking advantage or moving into unauthorized areas.

As you work with more departments and become familiar with their people and processes, you'll find ways to use their specialized knowledge in your business. Ask them who they use for print jobs, supplies, cleaning, or other tasks. Chances are they can look it up in their company's online database and save you the time and trouble of weeding out incompetent and dishonest vendors. Mine your client for industry reports, data, focus group findings, and other information that will enhance your knowledge of the industry. Many of the better reports are subscriber-based and very expensive. You probably don't subscribe to them; I never did. But as a supplier, you may find that your client will share these with you.

Look for ways to grow and learn from your client's knowledge base.

Help with Details

There are many other benefits your Elephant contacts can

provide to help you run your business more effectively and profitably:

Proven processes. As your company grows, you'll need to develop new processes. Examine your Elephant's processes—not just the nuts and bolts, but the principles behind them. You will pick up ideas that can help your growing business. For example, when I discovered the need for a procurement program for one of my first businesses, I sat down with the purchasing contact at my best Elephant and picked his brain. Like most people, he was eager to help. He told me everything he knew and gave me documents I could modify for use in my program. With the benefit of his big-business experience, I was able to set up a highly effective process quickly and inexpensively.

Discounts. Once you start getting substantial business from your Elephants, you can ask to use their negotiated rates when traveling on business for them. If you're in Seattle to call on Starbucks, you might be able to use their negotiated car rental and hotel rates, which I'm guessing are lower than yours. Make sure to get their approval first, usually through the purchasing department.

Use of facilities. Doing a lot of work for your Elephant, but wasting hours traveling? See if you can use a conference room or an empty office while getting work done for them. If you can also use their cafeteria, you might end up not only saving gas money but getting a better meal in the bargain. You might even score a contractor's badge, which can give you wider access and less scrutiny as you visit clients and prospects in the company. But don't take advantage of any special privileges—losing an Elephant's trust can be hazardous to your financial health.

Whether you own or operate a marketing company, mortgage brokerage firm, restaurant, print shop, or shoe store—and whether you run your business out of an office, in your home, or with a laptop and a cell phone at Starbucks—the time and effort you devote to leveraging your relationship with large clients can catapult your business through the roof.

Part V
FIVE KILLER MISTAKES

Mismanaging
Client
Expectations

He Said, She Said

S o here's the situation: you've implemented the first of what you hope will be many orders from your Elephant. As far as you can tell, everything went great—your business delivered the product on time and at the right price.

Now it's time to collect that pat on the back from your overjoyed client—and start working on your next project. Off you go to visit your new customer.

You walk into his office and—what's this? He's not overjoyed. He's not even mildly pleased. In fact, he seems to be in the middle of a slow burn.

What's the problem?

The problem, he says, is that he was really expecting you to deliver the goods earlier and for a lower price.

You're a bit taken aback. Why would he think such a thing?

Then you remember—when you were doing that full-court press to get him to sign, he asked you about your ability to beat the specified price and delivery deadline. You replied that your business usually beats both. You didn't mean to imply that it would *always* happen, with *every* order, but that's the way he took it.

There it is. An expectation that couldn't be met. A few more of those, and your Elephant will sprout wings and fly away.

How Does It Happen?

A vast majority of salespersons, including me in the past, tend to overpromise during the selling phase, figuring it'll help them get the business. Most of the time, however, this comes back to bite them. The reason is simple. Either they are just posturing for the sale and haven't checked their statements, or they fail to pass along their promises to those who can deliver on them—the operations staff. These people work to facilitate the contract according to its criteria and some direction from management. The result is predictable, and a bit sad. The only chance the company has of meeting the customer's expectations is by sheer luck.

Often the result is no repeat business. If the unmet expectation is serious enough, the company may even demand a refund. You don't have much leverage, especially at the beginning of what you hope will become a long-term relationship.

Here's the funny thing about expectations: more often than not, the unrealistic expectations that salespeople set are about things the customer didn't bring up and doesn't even care about. But once the customer has been led to expect a particular outcome, she'll hold your company accountable.

Fire Prevention

It's your instinct as a salesperson to be aggressively positive and persuasive about the product or service you're selling.

But there's a big difference between showing a "can do" spirit and making promises you're not absolutely sure you or your business can keep. Your goal should be to acquire for your business a reputation for overdelivering—and to get the reputation, you need to underpromise, while still presenting an attractive offer for your Elephant. Here's how:

Think before you speak. Don't get nervous about making the sale and let rhetoric override reason. Starting with your very first sentence, think about what you're going to say and how your customer might hear it. If you're not sure, repeat your claim or promise so that both parties understand.

Cut yourself some slack. Which contract issues are most important? Your client's priorities should become apparent to you as you put together and negotiate the contract. These are the very items on which you should underpromise—and overdeliver.

Define success. Do you know what the customer will consider fulfillment of the contract? Will success be measured by how much he paid and when the product was delivered? Return on investment? If so, what formula is he using? Whatever the measure, you need to understand clearly what information he's going to use to gauge his satisfaction with the contract. Make note of all questions and concerns that arise during your discussions. Use your intuition, too; sometimes the real concerns are never spoken.

Many Elephants use ROI (return on investment) to measure

Ole Alligator Mouth

If you say this but can't deliver, you're overpromising:

- "Our product will outperform everything else you're doing."
- "I guarantee you'll increase your business by 10 percent."
- "You can reach me anytime—I'm always available."
- "We have the best service in the industry, with 24-hour turnaround."
- "We'll have the latest and greatest in innovation."

Stand and Be Counted

One business I consulted with a few years back was Ryason Events, a company that charged its clients money for promoting their products and services through events staged in front of huge venues such as the Super Bowl, Spring Break, and the Indianapolis 500. They set up tents, hired performers, and produced shows.

Ryason's big customers measured marketing success in absolute terms. How much did the program shape the purchasing habits of the target audience? How many of the target audience actually attended the events?

Although most marketing companies offer market research as part of their programs, most Elephants prefer to engage third-party market research firms to implement the research. That's what one of them did after Ryason performed some contracted services for it.

The first research project yielded unacceptable results. Purchase levels and other measures were off, and Ryason didn't understand why. Didn't the program work? The results were so far below the customer's expectations that Ryason was in danger of being dropped by all its accounts in that company.

The research showed that fewer than 10 percent of the people surveyed remembered attending the event. We knew that couldn't be right. Something didn't make sense. We persuaded Ryason's customer to share the results.

A bit of digging and analysis got us to the bottom of things. The third-party research firm had used its standard method, which was to call everyone who lived in certain zip codes where the event had been held. But we had never intended to reach everyone in the area, only people who had attended the event.

The research firm and our client had made a huge mistake in methodology—one that could have killed my client's company right then and there. They had failed to get names and contact information from people who had been there in order to accurately measure the effectiveness of the program.

We had no choice but to persuade Ryason's big customer to run another study; we did this by agreeing to share the cost. Had we failed to persuade Ryason's Elephant, the invalid research data would have circulated throughout the company, and we would have been fighting it for a long time.

The correct methodology proved our program a success. The new data helped us gain much-needed credibility, which we were able to convert into more business. Had we not gotten involved and become part of the success criteria, we could have been dead in the water.

project success. Your contact probably plugs sales or revenue data into a software model set up to calculate ROI. You can be sure that one component of ROI will be a purchase measure (for example, an increase in profits resulting from a rise in sales, against the cost of your services) to determine whether the project worked. Your job is to find out exactly how your client measures ROI—specifically, which inputs (sales, profits, pricing) they use—then cover your bases in each area. Keep in mind that slight improvements in a well-chosen area can have a large positive impact on ROI.

Stay hands-on. Once you understand how success is being measured, make sure you cover every legitimate angle so that you have the greatest chance for success. Don't just put the contract in the In basket and walk away; follow through on every aspect of product or service specification and delivery. And pay close attention to how the customer is receiving and evaluating information about the results.

Perfect your processes. A good way to ensure that you can deliver on your customer's expectations is to use processes specifically designed to meet those expectations. Did you promise the procurement department that you'd keep track of the total amount of business you're doing with your customer, broken out by specific categories? Then you need to set up a system to provide that information— a computer program, perhaps, or maybe just a simple calculation from your accountant or finance department. You also need to develop a template form that you can share with your customer contact.

Although this one request may not be a big deal, rest assured that to fully manage your customer's expectations you'll probably have to create many such processes. Be careful to anticipate these—and include their costs in your price.

Communicate promises. Make sure all promises made to the customer are noted and passed along to the appropriate people in your business. As part of your weekly big-customer company meeting (see chapter 3, The Big-Company Focus), have the salesperson who made the sale walk the group through the details, including any promises that might have been implied or expectations that might have been created. Leave space on your customer contract details form for expectations and success criteria; this will remind your sales rep to get this critical information.

Pre-chart overdeliverables. When preparing for a sale, write down at least three items you can overdeliver—that is, parts of the contract in which you are confident you can do better than promised. During negotiations, look for issues of primary and secondary importance to the client, making sure you're crystal clear on how they view success in these areas.

Once you know which items matter most to your client, work hands-on to ensure that the people in your company who are responsible for delivering on them do everything possible to overdeliver. Then make sure the customer knows that you have achieved—indeed, surpassed—what you promised to do.

> **Make sure the customer knows that you have achieved—indeed, surpassed—what you promised to do.**

There are several ways of getting the good news to the customer, depending on the nature of your business and the item promised. If low price is the key deliverable and your charges are based on volume purchased, you can keep track of purchases and deliveries and continually share the information—including the unit price—with the customer. Use a simple, one-page contract status report showing pricing tiers with required volumes, and include information on what you've done to help the customer achieve or surpass the expected level.

Another method is to show the client the savings he has realized. If your regular pricing is $150,000 but you've charged only $110,000, draw attention to the $40,000 discount you're giving. This will help ensure future sales after the customer's program review, as well as bolster your contact's annual employee review.

If receiving your product or service on time is a critical issue, at regular intervals send the customer a status sheet listing date ordered, production time, and delivery date to specified locations. Your client will love getting this information before his own people can get it to him.

Fumbling
Client Crises

Blindsided by Sudden Catastrophe

Of course, all that booming sales activity increases the risk that you'll be drawn into a crisis involving your client—a crisis that can be pivotal in shaping your future relationships. Although you never wish for bad things to happen, one positive result of dealing successfully with a debacle is that you prove yourself worthy of a client's trust and confidence.

Cleaning Up

A client wanted to use one of our marketing programs to test the distribution of samples of a cleaning product. The plan was to distribute the sample, along with a safety booklet, to parents as they arrived at school for parent-teacher conferences. It seemed like a pretty simple plan—until four school principals called me fuming because the samples were leaking and the cleaner had spilled all over their floors.

We sprang into action. First, I informed Debbie, our client, that the packaging might be faulty. Then I hired a telemarketing firm to call each of the 100 schools participating in the test and ask officials to check the shipment. More than a quarter of the shipments were, in fact, leaking. We immediately sent our local shippers to those schools to pick up the shipments and, if possible, help clean up the mess. We then contacted each school and sent a $100 donation along with a profuse apology.

After that, I put together a detailed action sheet outlining the problem, the steps I had taken to solve it, and the cost (about $7,000). As it turned out, the adhesive used in the packaging dissolved when exposed to the cleaner. Because the whole problem arose from our client's faulty packaging, it was obvious who was at fault.

I sent the action sheet to Debbie, who called me immediately. She was pleased with how we had handled this potential catastrophe, noting that most suppliers would have either swept the problem under the rug or left the mess for her to deal with.

Debbie was even more impressed when I told her that we would cover the costs.

Yes, the client would have been happy to pay the charges, but to do so would have meant filling out paperwork and amending the project budget, thus tying her to this problem. Knowing this, I figured that the $7,000 would buy me ten times that much in goodwill. In fact, I was right, and word got out that ours was a company that looked after its champions. When the product was launched, the client asked us to run the national program. They also gave us a lot more work.

Down the Hatch

I can remember the exact moment when I got the call. A client who manufactured and marketed a mouthwash wanted us to distribute product samples to teenagers in high schools. We designed what we thought was a clever sampling program: each student would be given a bag with a mouthwash sample and, for inspiration, a sixteen-page booklet extolling the value of motivation. We also put together a contest in which students who created songs and videos on the motivation theme would compete for a trip to Los Angeles to produce their song at a major studio. Sounds harmless enough, right?

Around 2:30 one Friday afternoon, my client, Alex, called in a panic. A student had discovered that the samples contained alcohol and had gone on a mouthwash binge. Going to his last class, he collided with the door and vomited in the middle of the classroom.

I was shocked. None of us had given a second's thought to checking the amount of alcohol in these little samples. How much could they really contain?

I told Alex to take a deep breath; then I called the school principal. The principal remained calm as he filled me in on the details. Apparently the student drank a whopping twenty-nine samples of mouthwash. He told the other students that he had been shooting for fifty but had to stop.

The principal assured me that the student was okay and that his parents weren't the litigious type. After seeking some legal advice anyway, I spoke to the teenager's parents. They were not at all amused by their son's behavior and actually apologized to me for his ruining the program for the rest of the school.

I knew it was time to implement an official policy on what types of product samples we'd deliver to consumers. I flew to see Alex and was able to save my neck by presenting our new criteria for products: no drugs, no alcohol, and no glass containers.

Alex, taken off guard by my vigorous crisis management, was completely satisfied. I knew that before he or others in his division could continue to do business with us, he would need to see that we had taken steps to change the way we operated. The key was to take responsibility for the drunken student episode, even though there wasn't much we could have done about it, and to implement official, written policy changes at my own small company.

You Did What?

One of my salespeople once told me that, the day before, he had accidentally put some documents in the wrong overnight courier package. "It's not the end of the world," I told him. "Just ask them to send it back, and we'll get the papers out to the right people tomorrow."

Then he dropped the bombshell: the document was a contract loaded with details on a client's new product. Even worse, the person to whom the salesperson accidentally sent it was another client who just happened to be a fierce competitor of the first client.

Our reputation for keeping our clients' secrets was at stake. After I picked myself up off the floor, we mapped out a plan. Calling the courier wasn't an option, because the package had already been delivered to the competitor's mailroom.

Growing desperate, I considered calling people at the receiving client's office to needle them into confiscating the package. After several tries, I finally got hold of the client's secretary, whom I didn't know very well. I babbled my way through a speech about why she should take the overnight package off my client's desk and destroy it. After several minutes of persuasion, she relented.

The next day I sent her a gift basket of cookies. The mutually beneficial interaction strengthened our relationship with her, and she became much more helpful to us in setting appointments with her superiors.

Mind Your P's and Q's

Now for a crisis right on the firing line. I was working with my team on the final presentation in a promotion for a candy company that was considering two other agencies. We were the last to present our stuff. Our proposed program had a pro-football theme; we called it THE BIG PASS.

The night before the presentation, which was scheduled for 9:00 in the morning, my staff and I worked until well after midnight. At 3:00 AM, all that remained to be finished was our PowerPoint presentation, which needed to be touched up a bit. One of my employees volunteered to stay to complete it.

About an hour before the meeting, I arrived at the office bleary-eyed to find the employee frantically finishing the presentation. At 8:45, he said he was finished. The prospective clients came in and sat down with some coffee and bagels to view our brilliant plan.

I was presenting first for our team, so I prepped the room before turning on the projector, which would reveal our vivid graphics and colorful logo for THE BIG PASS. Our clients perched on the edge of their seats.

I turned off the lights, flipped the projector switch—and heard the room explode in guffaws.

There on the screen, in two-foot-tall letters, shone the great new logo we had created:

THE BIG ASS

Obviously the late hours had got to our typist, but that provided little consolation. Nor did it help when I noticed that THE BIG ASS was embedded in the template, which meant that it was on the lower right corner of every slide.

After the laughter died down, I said, "That's no typo—we wanted to promote the candy's dubious nutritional value in our campaign." Everyone must have been in a good mood, because the room once again erupted in laughter. We went on to finish the presentation without further incident.

We got the account. The client later told me part of the reason: they were impressed we weren't distracted by the screw-up. Sheer luck is more like it, I'd say.

Steve, Help!

Here's an example of a crisis with no real resolution. A number of years ago, I was working to capture a new client, a chewing gum company. At the time, we had only one other client, so the stakes were high. The buyer, Sherry, liked our ideas and wanted to hire us to run a large sampling program. She mentioned one obstacle: because gum is considered a food, her company would have to check the quality of the facility we were using to pack the samples into the carrying bags to be given to consumers. Her company would pack only in completely sterile facilities, but she assured me that as long as the packing plant was safe and clean, all would be fine.

As a favor, Sherry gave me the checklist of criteria that would be used to rate our facility. Like any good salesperson, I passed it along to the person who selected facilities for us. He assured me we had nothing to worry about, because our packing person had been doing this sort of work for years. I assumed that everything was good to go.

In the next room, I was greeted with a "Steve, over here." Down on the floor were rodent droppings.

That was my first mistake.

As I pulled up to the facility, a beat-up building crying out for some security, I knew I was in trouble. Sherry and her entourage arrived and began the tour. The first thing I noticed was a dingy water mark about two feet above the floor. We were told that there had recently been a flood but it was now under control.

In the next room, I was greeted with a "Steve, over here." Down on the floor were rodent droppings.

Believe it or not, the tour went downhill from there.

Around 3 PM, Sherry, who was just under five feet tall and weighed about ninety pounds, was walking down the hall toward the rest of us when a bell rang. Suddenly, 150 workers got up and rushed up the hall, sweeping Sherry along with them. My last memory of Sherry that day is of her yelling, "Steve! Help!" No one had bothered to tell us that at 3 PM sharp all the workers run to board their bus for home.

Needless to say, we didn't get the business that day. We did, however, hire a new person to direct our facilities. It took us several years to recover from that fiasco with that particular Elephant. I did hear from Sherry, though, who left a message thanking me for the biggest laugh she'd had in years.

Lessons

So much for disaster stories. They're exciting, yes—gripping, often funny, especially if they're somebody else's disaster. But disaster stories have morals, too. Here are the key points I've learned in dealing with the inevitable client crisis.

Do whatever it takes to fix it. The future business you stand to make or lose almost always outweighs the cost of dealing with the immediate crisis.

Take responsibility, no matter whose fault it was. You can take part of the blame, but never none of it. In almost every crisis there is something you could have done which would have averted the problem.

Act swiftly and effectively. Don't just hope the problem will go away by itself. Sometimes people just want to vent their anger and be heard, and swift action will often put out the fire. Be a good ear, express concern for the client's situation, then try to close off the issue. Most people are programmed to expect a "not my fault" response. Try a simple apology; this usually does the trick.

Step in and take charge. Don't rely on the person who caused the crisis to manage it competently. Everyone likes to deal with stand-up people, and big customers are no different. True character surfaces under duress. Use the crisis to prove yourself.

Don't assign blame. Ass covering and finger pointing can only diminish you in the eyes of others. The client is more interested in how the crisis is handled than in who caused the problem.

Stay calm. Deal with the crisis in ways that will make you friends, not enemies. Maintain your poise and your sense of humor; it will help your client do the same. Use the opportunity to close ranks with your client as you work together toward a solution. Your ability to keep your composure and lead will rule the day.

Communicate. Stay in close touch with the client; be reassuring if you can, but never lie or cover up. Once your client becomes aware of the crisis, the worst thing you can do is not keep her fully informed. Understand that her boss and other departments will probably be asking questions. You don't want to put her in an "I don't know" position—she'll never forgive you for it.

Keep your eye on the ball. Even when up to your big pass in alligators, don't lose sight of your larger goals: the success of this project, and winning future contracts.

Remember that your clients know the occasional snafu is bound to happen; what they're watching for is how you'll handle it.

Closure

Big companies are process machines. They have protocols, policies, and processes for everything—and they expect you to have them as well. Most of you don't understand this; I didn't. If you don't resolve an outstanding unexplained negative issue, it festers until it's insurmountable and perhaps fatal. Get on top of it *now*. Create a standard action plan for bringing crises to an end.

> **Your clients know the occasional snafu is bound to happen; what they're watching for is how you'll handle it.**

If the crisis originated in your business, make the changes needed to ensure that it will never happen again. It's not enough to say that you're going to do things differently in the future or that you'll make sure it never happens again. *Document the crisis*—by writing up a process report, for instance.

After my first crisis, I drew up a process revision form, a simple document with three sections: Problem, Current Process, and Changes to Current Process. In the first section I'd outline the problem that had occurred— not to assign blame, but to document whatever mistakes had been made. The middle section would be used to describe the actions that had led to the problem or that had allowed it to happen, along with how we had handled the problem. In the final section I'd list the changes we were making in our processes to ensure that the problem wouldn't occur again.

I'd give this report to my client contact to help her address any issues raised by her company's senior management. We would also pass it along to other departments, such as purchasing and consumer relations, that inevitably hear about every problem you have, many of whom can kill your deal (chapter 4). The report provides information they need and usually stops any investigations that might affect your status as an approved supplier.

As you can see, keeping your big customer happy is no easy chore, but it will pay off handsomely over the years if you cultivate your reputation as a stand-up problem solver. Elephants are risk-averse. If they feel that dealing with your company is less risky than dealing with your competitors because you're a stand-up person with good policies and processes, that's what they'll do. And the longer you stay on your Elephant's good side, the more your sales increase—along with your profit margin.

Operational Explosion

Biting Off More Than You Can Chew

You worked hard, you put in long hours, you sold like crazy, and you bagged your Elephant. Your business is cooking on all burners and may even have exceeded your sales objectives. Why, then, you ask, is your business falling apart?

Let me ask *you* a question: What happens when you put ten pounds of potatoes in a one-pound bag?

Success^2 = Failure

Melinda sold for Anson Ltd., a corrugated box brokerage company owned by Bob Anson. The company's customers were local small businesses.

Anson Ltd. grew weary of struggling to make ends meet, so the company embarked on a Bag the Elephant strategy. Melinda was very committed and did everything needed to reach the objective.

After six months of hard work, Melinda brought in the good news: Anson would now be supplying the boxes for the largest gift retailer in the U.S. The contract would, in the first year alone, more than double Anson's annual sales, and Melinda's personal sales record increased more than tenfold. Pretty awesome!

The new client's requirements brought changes in Anson's processes: a smaller window between order and delivery, and a larger distribution area, regional instead of local. All ordering had to be communicated through a single procurement manager at the client's headquarters. Normally this would be fine, but in this case the logistics also had to be coordinated at each of the regional locations receiving the boxes. Melinda communicated this to the owner, and Bob was fine with the requirements, figuring that the increase in cash and manufacturing volume would more than make up for the extra cost. He figured, as do many owners, that he'd get the sale—then deal with the execution issues later.

The problem with this course of action is that your Elephant demands better than perfect service—and wants it *now!*

Your Elephant isn't interested in the fact that you haven't prepared for the increase in business. Elephants tend to be highly attuned to operational issues at the beginning of the contract, and chances are your salesperson has spent a lot of time reassuring the Elephant that you can easily handle its needs, better even than its most recent vendor. Unrealistic

---

Take Responsibility for What You Sell

If you're a salesperson, you have a big-time vested interest in the delivery of the item you sold. Don't take the attitude, "I've done my job, now let the others do theirs." If you expect any additional business from your Elephant, you must back up the promises you've made. If you don't, you can kiss any new business goodbye. Believe me, it's much better for your survival to figure out what operational issues the new business might present and deal with them up front, before the sale is made. Don't hide behind your operations manager or owner—take responsibility for the things you sell and the promises you make. Take a stand, and if your owner or manager isn't considering how the new business will impact the organization, suggest strongly that she do so.

expectations set by a salesperson, a supplier company unprepared for the heavy workload—this is a recipe for disaster.

To meet the customer's expectations, Bob agreed to several first-time activities. He would carry inventory. Until then, they had been reluctant to do so for fear of being stuck with material that didn't sell. Bob was a broker, and anything he couldn't move he would have to eat.

Bob hired five customer service representatives to handle the ordering and logistics with the customer's regional offices. Even with these measures, Anson began to run into trouble once the orders started coming in. Deliveries were late, and many that arrived on time contained the wrong box sizes. Since the shipping was now regional, Anson was a smaller player; it lacked the clout to pressure the shipping companies to deliver its material expeditiously.

As time went on, the customer became more and more incensed with what it considered unacceptable service, and Melinda had to bear the brunt of the Elephant's wrath. Bob threw more and more resources at the problem. He pulled key people off his core business to help. This only made the problem worse. Now, not only the new customer but all customers were unhappy. Then Bob's employees began to get concerned, and morale dropped to an all-time low.

At one point, Bob actually considered closing up shop. He was spending so much trying to execute for this one Elephant that his business was losing money. That's right: double the sales volume, but negative profits for the entire year—a tough lesson, to be sure!

Bob and Melinda struggled for some time before they figured things out. Unfortunately, by this time Anson's Elephant had gotten away. Melinda lost out on a potential windfall, but Bob did manage to save most of his core local clients.

Everyone learned a big lesson from this experience, and the company has never repeated the mistake. As part of the quotes for new Elephants, Anson has its operations and salespersons plan exactly how they are going to deliver on the new business. Since then, Melinda and Bob have gone on to bag several Elephants, and the business is doing well. But I know that today Bob considers himself lucky that he still has his business.

What's Happening?

To ensure that you don't fall victim to this fatal mistake, let's begin by outlining a series of increasingly dire signs that your business has bitten off more than it can chew:

1. Customer expectations aren't being met.
2. Your business goes into reaction mode to try to save the account.
3. Resources (money and people) are drawn from other parts of your business.
4. The customer is upset, your business goes into panic mode, and employee morale takes a hit.
5. Your preexisting business suffers from reallocation of resources.
6. Profits head south.
7. The customer takes a hike.
8. Your business tries to pick up the pieces.

Pretty bleak, huh? Who would've thought that getting a huge customer could actually be a death sentence? Believe it or not, half the battle is keeping yourself from falling into the "I'll focus on the sale now and deal with the operational issues later" mentality. If you do, take heed—you're inviting disaster.

Mock Elephant Plan

The mistake of underplanning is common in Elephant country. Sometimes you see it in time to avoid it, sometimes you don't. I used to wing it, figuring that I'd deal with delivering the goods once I had the sale, but I sometimes paid the price. I've watched many a bagged Elephant break away and disappear into the distance.

Based on my experience and others' in the School of Hard Knocks, I've put together a six-step method for avoiding this trap. I call it my Mock Elephant Plan. I've used this plan countless times, and it's been a lifesaver.

Now, I'm not suggesting that you implement the Mock

Elephant Plan every time you sell something. However, the exercise should be performed

- whenever you attempt to dramatically increase your sales levels in a short time,
- whenever you alter the product or service you sell, or
- whenever a promise is made to an Elephant that might impact the way you do things—offering reduced pricing for a volume buy (your business must deal with the increase in volume) or promising to ship regionally when your previous shipping was local (your business might have to deal with a different shipping company).

The Mock Elephant Plan must be executed at the quote stage, *before* you get the account. Afterwards just might be too late.

Step 1: Bring the Gang

Have a meeting, and be sure to include everyone involved in any stage of fulfilling the potential contract. It doesn't matter whether you have two employees or two hundred—have the right people there. Aside from solid operational execution, this will accomplish at least two desirable things:

- Your employees will love the fact that they had input and will embrace any increased workload caused by the Elephant, because they were part of it—it wasn't forced on them.
- You're less likely to overlook important issues and procedures, because good department heads will know their tasks better than you.

The meetings don't need to be long, just effective. Get to the point. Have the sales contact walk through the opportunity, making sure to include any promises she's already made or priority issues important to the potential customer. Then proceed to the operational review step.

Step 2: Review Operations

Depending on the size and complexity of your business, this step can be short or long, but it needs to happen.

Write down every step your company must take in order to meet the current business operational needs. Begin with the signing of the contract, then walk through each department's current requirements. To simplify this procedure, I drew up a step-by-step flow chart showing how my company executed its core business. Because most of your business execution will be similar, chances are you'll have to draw up the basic chart only once, but if you keep it up to date, it will work for about 90 percent of your sales.

Step 3: Anticipate Problems

Think about what the increase in business might do to each step from your operational review. What about an increase in sales volume? Will it strain your existing staff? Will you need to buy more materials? What about delivery or store hours? Every step in your company's process must be discussed. By running through the operational steps sequentially, you'll reassure yourself that you haven't forgotten anything. Identify areas where your current way of doing things just won't work for this new opportunity. Look for potential problems by poking holes in the current system. Ask yourself "what if" questions, then create action steps to mitigate those problems.

Step 4: Communicate

This step—think of it as baby-sitting your Elephant—is often overlooked but essential to success. Here's what you have to do:

- Meet the needs of your big customer on the current job.
- Start interacting more with Resource and Necessity departments as you learn who they are.
- Keep your champions cheering.
- Keep a sharp eye on new opportunities that may emerge from your relationship with this new customer. Ask yourself, What else can this sale lead to?

All this coordination takes people and process. Work as a team to set up the most effective system. Do you need account service or customer service staff to communicate with your Elephant's resource staff directly? Do you have enough personnel? In order to land as much business as possible, take a look at your sales presence in the company; you might need to add a person or two. I revised my account team every six months or so to handle my growing business.

Pay attention to the communication issue. Get as many of your people talking and working with as many of your customer's people as possible. When restructuring your resources to handle your Elephant's business, maintain continuity so the customer gets comfortable relying on the same people.

Look at how you share information internally as well. Do you need anything more, such as software, to facilitate communication? How about dinner meetings or other set times for the Elephant team to meet?

Step 5: Include Costs in Quote

I'm sure you've figured out by now where I'm going with steps one through four. They are all critical in avoiding an operational crunch, and they also cost money. Now, here's the step that keeps you from giving away all of your profits: for each new action step you have to add, capture the associated costs—*and include them in your quote.*

You may need dedicated customer service people with unique training, customized order forms, more suppliers, increased inventory, raw materials, more visits to the client, and many other things that cost money. The Mock Elephant Plan allows you to deal with these things *now* and include them in your price. Otherwise you'll pay for them later out of your profits. Even if you choose to split or eat the costs, at least you'll know what they are before you walk off the cliff.

Had Bob implemented the plan, he and his salesperson, Melinda, would have known that they needed to make changes in operations. He would have charged the customer for them; the customer probably would have been happy with the service; Anson would have actually made money; and the disaster would have been avoided.

Another option would have been to omit some of the services that the Elephant did not need when selling to the prospect in the first place. This way, Anson wouldn't have had to deliver on them and could have brought more to the bottom line.

Step 6: Have a Backup Plan

The last step in the Mock Elephant Plan is for the skeptic— that's me! Once you've completed steps one through five, ask yourself what the biggest issues or crippling problems might be. Perhaps, like Anson, you've promised delivery regionally. If that is a customer priority, a backup plan should be developed in case of a misadventure. Your team's ability to identify as many potential minefields as possible, and have backup plans for them, can make the difference between an operational disaster and a healthy, growing business.

The Elephant Trap

All Your Eggs in One Basket

Your Elephant is dancing all around you, and you can't believe how well you're doing. You're getting more business from your Elephant than you ever thought possible; your sales staff are going crazy with big-time commissions; you've hired more quality people, expanded your services, and even moved into new markets. Not only are your salespeople getting rich, you're making a bucketload of cash, too. Things are so good that you're putting money down on a new car and maybe even a new house. Life is great!

Then the phone rings.

It's your champion—a great guy, a prince who's become your dearest friend and your children's godfather.

"We've decided to switch suppliers," he says. "We're changing our company strategy, and we don't require your services anymore. But thanks for the past three years. Good luck." Click.

You've suddenly gone hollow, and the words echo inside you. You see everything you've built coming apart in an instant. You've been blindsided.

What happened?

Client dependency. Having grown comfortable with the regular arrival of armored-carloads of cash, you've left yourself exposed and vulnerable.

Frantic, you try to contact competing Elephants to see if they might need your services—now that you've got time for them. But you haven't done any reconnaissance or preselling, so once again, you're out of luck.

You've got no choice. You have to cut costs and try to pull off a miracle. The first to go are employees who were hired specifically to work on the Elephant; then, if the bleeding doesn't stop, others, including valued employees who have been with you for years.

The pain grows more intense. You've been neglecting your base clientele, your smaller, less glamorous customers, and they've been drifting away unnoticed—until now. You've got next to nothing left in the customer department.

So—what *do* you have left? A huge inventory, lots of new equipment, rental contracts you can't break. And very few people to help pull you out of the ditch.

Ssshhh! It Happens

As I can personally attest, it's easy to become Elephant dependent. It happened to me with Procter & Gamble, the very client I'm using as my central example.

Once I started cookin' with P&G, things went really fast. My Elephant was shaking the money tree, and even though my sales force and I were trying hard to bag other Elephants, the success we were having at P&G dwarfed all our other business. Obviously, this was great—we definitely needed the business—but the downside was that it left us almost completely dependent on this one Elephant. It was a situation that took me several anxiety-filled years to fix.

The total company and sales effort put forth to bag an Elephant is huge. Ideally, your entire business is on the same page, working strenuously to target a few high-value prospects. But regardless, here's what happens:

- After a while, you start to have some success with the prospect.
- A small contract is signed, and everybody in your business celebrates.
- While this is going on, you or your salespeople have been trying to secure other big customers, with little success.
- If you're a salesperson, you might be inclined to follow the path of least resistance and try to sell new accounts in the big company. It's human nature—the commissions are better there—but it accelerates your business toward dependency.
- You devote great attention to the first contract and work your way through with no problems. However, you notice that if you made a few adjustments to your standard operating procedures, you'd do a better job of meeting the needs of your Elephant. These changes might include increased or enhanced services, dedication of specific employees to the Elephant account, or maybe even some cost-cutting in exchange for a volume order.
- Because you've seen firsthand how the Elephant operates, the changes are effective, which leads to more and more business.
- Time goes on, relationships build, your business keeps evolving to meet the needs of your one big customer. Even more business comes your way. Perhaps, with the help of your Elephant, you've even expanded your core business into other areas. The next thing you know, sales are booming! The only problem: one customer represents 70 percent or more of your business. (The same thing holds true if you're a salesperson. If you've become dependent on one customer for your sales, you, too, are vulnerable.)

Why is Elephant dependency bad? Well, leaving aside for a moment the crippling loss of revenues and profits that can happen when the Elephant bolts and goes over the horizon, being Elephant dependent can result in the following:

Poor negotiating position. Your Elephant will probably know how important it is to you. If the customer has a procurement program for vendors, part of the periodic auditing process is a review of your business's finances. P&G used to simply compare my company's total revenues with the amounts it paid to us. The result: Elephant power!

Guilt by association. Depending on the customer, other Elephants may not want to play with you. If you become known as an appendage of the big customer, a position you definitely are *not* shooting for, competitors may be wary of working with you in fear of confidential information reaching your larger customer.

Keeping Things in Balance

What's the best customer mix? I'm asked this question all the time. Unfortunately, there's no simple, one-size-fits-all answer. It depends on the industry, the economy, the size of your company, the size of the Elephant, the color of your car, and myriads of other factors.

You'd think the best situation would be to have as many customers as possible, but that's not always the case. When your company is smaller or just starting out, the stability and growth opportunities provided by a big customer are immensely valuable, and you should seek this dependency. It may make the difference between sailing and sinking.

The trick is to *use the relationship to your advantage.* Build a solid business foundation, then move to protect yourself from the negative ramifications of one-customer dependency by adding other customers to dilute the power of your Elephant.

If you're trying to sell your business, without question your best position is to have the lowest single-customer concentration you can manage. This gives a buyer confidence that the business can succeed should it lose a customer or two in the transition.

If your business is small but plateaued out and you have no desire to grow it, that's okay. But first you should seek to reduce your customer dependency to protect yourself against a big hit should they leave. And if you find yourself dramatically overdependent, don't fret. There are actions you can take.

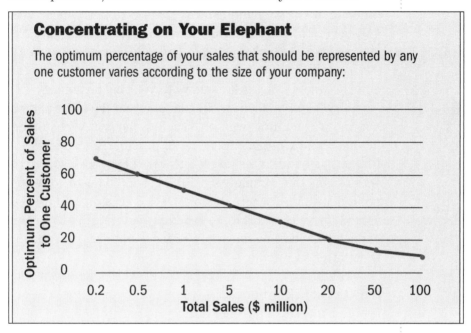

Concentrating on Your Elephant

The optimum percentage of your sales that should be represented by any one customer varies according to the size of your company:

Protecting Yourself

Sometimes it's great to be entrenched in one big company. In a perfect world, you'd be deeply codependent with your Elephant, but instead of the big customer having all the power, you'd be able to protect yourself. The world is not perfect, of course, but here are some key strategies that can help you achieve a measure of protection.

Keep your ear to the ground. Nothing is more important than information. If you know what's going on behind the scenes with your customer, you have a huge advantage. Not only can you use this knowledge to generate business, it can also give you advance warning of the chopping block, giving you time to reposition or conduct damage control.

If you've cultivated the key relationships and the people you're dealing with are getting value from you, they'll want to protect you by making sure you're not replaced. After all, you're their key to information within their own company.

Reinvent yourself. Another benefit of knowing what's going on is that you should have excellent intelligence about your Elephant's future plans. What are senior managers thinking about your industry as they look to the next year and beyond? What are their new objectives? What are the new buzzwords they're using to describe and gauge success? If you don't reinvent yourself at the right times, you can quickly become yesterday's news to your big customer.

At P&G I remember vividly that one year the focus of their marketing spending was on reaching as many customers in the brand's target audience as possible. Terms such as "broadscale" and "mass targeting" were being used. Only two years later, the company's thinking had changed to "entry point marketing," where the focus was on customers entering a new target—for instance, reaching younger teens versus older teens because the younger teens will be teens longer, thus better customers.

While nearly all of my competitors were coming out with their broadscale products, my company adopted P&G's POME (point of market entry) marketing program. Needless to say, it wasn't even close. We walked away with the lion's share of the business—all because we knew where the Elephant was going and we got there first.

Be stingy with exclusivity. If you give exclusivity— meaning that you can't offer the product or service to any of your customer's competitors—try to define "competitor" as narrowly as possible. Make sure, as well, that you charge a premium for the exclusivity and that you keep leveraging the price of exclusivity every time your contract comes up for renewal. Not only does it help keep your bottom line healthy, it sends the message that other Elephants find you appealing as well.

Seek a multi-year commitment. Hedge against the Elephant's quick goodbye by getting your customer to sign a long-term contract. Often you'll have to give up something for this, but you can usually get something in return. You might ask for a three- to five-year contract at a 10 percent discount, but with substantially more volume than you would normally get. This would more than make up for the price reduction. Another advantage, as we'll see in the next chapter, is guaranteed long-term cash flow.

Spread your contracts. As you work your way through your big customer, try to capture contracts from as many different factions as possible. At the height of our business with P&G, we had more than fifty different contracts, spread across all three categories of company departments:

- The **Profit Holders** category had thirty different brand groups from four divisions (Food and Beverage, Healthcare, Personal Care, and Over the Counter Medicines).
- The **Necessity** category had four contracts for activities such as shipping and manufacturing. We also had four multi-year contracts across three different divisions.
- The **Resource** category had sixteen contracts spread across seven different resource group members, such as consumer relations, professional affairs, marketing operations, market research, and marketing services.

The important point here is that it would have been very hard for P&G to cut us off all at once. Though losing all that business would have been crippling, the loss would have been gradual, and we would have had some time to bail. The other point here is that everything works together, and the more champions and contracts you acquire throughout the company, the harder it is for the Elephant to get rid of you.

Price correctly. This one might sound silly, but make sure to turn a profit on the products and services you're offering. If you're making money, you can build a war chest for that rainy day.

Reducing Dependency

Now that your business is firing on all cylinders, it's time to reduce your dependency. The first thing to know is that you shouldn't ease up on the gas. Keep on getting as much as you can from your Elephant.

Since dependency is measured by the percentage of your total revenue or sales that comes from any one customer, you can reduce the percentage in one of two ways:

- Replace the big customer with another big customer.
- Increase your sales to another company.

Guess which one we're going to pursue. That's right: go out and get more sales from other big customers.

Here are some strategies to increase your chances of success with a new Elephant:

Replicate successful sales strategies. Elephants like each other—what's good for one is often good for others. If you've done your job, you've learned tons from your Elephant about measuring performance, navigating bureaucracy, handling company politics, gaining champions, and other skill sets. Use this knowledge to expedite the next Elephant.

> **Elephants like each other. What's good for one is often good for others.**

Analyze what worked best with your big customer, then try to reapply it without giving away any confidential information. Who else in the industry would appreciate the services you've perfected? Go forth and bag them. If there's something your current Elephant does that adds to and enhances your services, consider adding those procedures as part of your own service.

Leverage your credibility. Your involvement with your big customer should have given you great samples of your work, case studies, and so forth. If you can, share these with prospective customers. This will go far in getting them past the credibility issue they usually have with businesses they haven't used before. I know that when my salespeople showed prospects samples from work we did at P&G, we were immediately taken seriously.

Salesperson focus. This too might sound trite, but make new business top priority for all appropriate salespeople. Get the entire business on board, just as you did when you set out to bag your first Elephant.

Make a choice. At times you might need to choose between a current Elephant and a potential new big client. You'll have to be careful here, because you don't want to upset your Elephant, but that aside, you'd be wise to get started with a new prospect. At times a prospect's ability to take something away from the incumbent is enough for a sale. When faced with this situation, I always tried to get a compromise that would allow my company to get both the new and old customers. You may, however, need to be a bit creative in your options.

Keep a waiting list. If appropriate in your industry, keep a list of customers who want your product or service.

Big customers should be your ticket to massive success. The important thing is to not get blindsided.

Losing Sight of the Numbers

Up Cash Creek Without a Paddle

Business has never been better. You've bagged one Elephant already and are well on your way to getting another one. Your salespeople have really stepped up to the plate, and things are humming along better than you ever expected. You sit down for a minute and ponder just how great things are. For the first time, you think that big-time success is truly right around the corner—so close you can taste it.

But—what's that note by your phone? Someone has left a message: Call Accounting immediately.

Not a good sign.

You take a deep breath and make the call.

The news hits you like a punch in the stomach: you're all but out of money. Your employees might not get paid. The suppliers that you rely on so heavily for materials will be left twisting in the wind—

which might jeopardize your big-customer contract. All travel and entertainment must cease, which will kill your sales momentum. And it's a cinch you won't be taking your spouse to the Riviera this year, either.

Wait a minute. What's wrong with this picture? You're kicking butt at your huge customer. You've sold over $1 million in the past six months, and that's more than your entire last year. How could you be out of money?

At this point, your accountant could give you any of several reasons. But let's look at two of the most common scenarios when businesses are doing plenty of business but still going broke. The math is pretty basic: either (1) your customers are not paying in time for you to cover your own operating expenses, or (2) your customers are paying you on time, but your expenses are higher than you expected.

But which is it? What prompted your accountant to call you up and ruin your weekend? Let's take these possibilities one at a time.

> **You've sold over $1 million in the past six months, and that's more than your entire last year. How could you be out of money?**

Get Paid on Time

Your accountant tells you your biggest customer hasn't paid its invoices. You've sold $1 million, but you've collected almost none of it. This is obviously horrendous in its own right, but what makes matters even worse is that you've been paying your bills the whole time. It's pretty simple: lots of cash going out and not much coming in.

Most of the businesses and their owners I've known, including me, have at some point fallen prey to Forgetful Elephant Syndrome, which is often the diagnosis when the big customer simply doesn't pay its bills on time. In my case, it happened early in my career, and I got lucky—I collected some past-due payments before things got fatal. After this terrible experience, I became more vigilant about keeping cash on hand.

Cash is business fuel. It's the lifeblood of your company. Without it you can't exist, and if you're going to grow with your Elephant, it's vital that you understand how to get your customers to pay you on time. It's also imperative that you put together a contingency plan should you ever find yourself in this precarious situation. Here are the top three reasons why big companies pay late:

1. They are bureaucracies. (By now you've heard the bureaucracy complaint a million times, so you should be ready for it.) Every invoice that comes into a large company must follow a specific process for approval and payment. Until this process is complete, you're not getting paid.

2. They make money on your money. It's not unusual for big customers to pay anywhere from 90 to 120 days after receiving your invoice. Think about the vast river of cash that flows through a big company. Interest on a single day's cash outlays is substantial; multiply that by 90 to 120 and you see the economics at work. And do you ask them to pay you that interest? No? Why not? That's right. You don't want to upset them.

3. Because they can. They're bigger than you and can make you wait. It's as simple as that. Anyway, it makes no difference whether they're slow on purpose or because their gears grind slowly; either way, you're not getting paid.

You're not totally without options, though. There are things you can do to minimize your wait for the big company's vault door to swing open.

First, get your house in order. I'll bet most of you invoice late—a needless delay. Get your invoice on its way and start the countdown to payment as soon as possible. This might require you to revise or upgrade certain areas of your business, but do it anyway. It's that important. With one customer, we were required to send proof of service—usually from an independent audit—along with our invoice. We managed to adjust the audit procedure and its timing enough to bill two weeks earlier than before—which meant we got paid two weeks earlier, too.

Understand the customer's processes. Find out how payments are approved, where invoices should be sent, to whom they should be addressed, and how they should be formatted. This will save intracompany routing time and get your money to you faster.

Meet purchasing people. Find out who writes the checks, then find an excuse to meet that person or persons. Believe me, they have a thankless job, and your efforts will not go unrewarded. I used to tell the person who championed the contract that I wanted to make sure I had recorded all the company information correctly so she wouldn't have to chase it down later. This usually worked like a charm. Most people will gladly provide a name if it means less work for them later.

Get the numbers. When you get a contract signed, ask your Elephant whether a P.O. number or other internal code was issued. If so, get the number and include it on your invoice. That alone might save two weeks.

Know how to troubleshoot. Understand the procedure for checking on past-due invoices. (Usually this does not involve a call to your contact, which is something you want to avoid.) Check with the responsible party first. It's usually someone in purchasing or a lower-level employee in the department you contracted with. That person can tell you at what point in the company's ductwork your paperwork is moldering, and probably the exact date it's scheduled for payment. (In order to keep from looking like a small-timer, you should normally let your accounting department pursue past-due bills.)

> **In order to keep from looking like a small-timer, you should normally let your accounting department pursue past-due bills.**

Ask your contact. I don't recommend using your contact for this purpose very often. If you have to, it should be someone you are well acquainted with personally, because you never want to look anything but financially stable to your Elephant.

Invoice correctly. You should never have an invoice returned for lack of required information.

Mind Your Margins

What about the second scenario: lots of money coming in, a lot more money going out?

Let's say you've done what we suggested in chapter 10: you've stood up to your Elephant and negotiated what you believed to be favorable terms, good enough to ensure you a tidy profit. And yet you're losing money. How can this be happening?

I recently received a call from Don Jeter, owner of Barracuda Labs, a company that specializes in refurbishing used computer chips. Don was justly proud of his company's $20 million in annual sales, his fifty employees, his brand-new third office.

You'd expect someone like Don to be cleaning up. Appearances, unfortunately, masked a company in deep peril. Barracuda might have been taking in $20 million, but it was spending more than that each year just to operate. Why? As it turns out, Don had failed to factor in certain fixed operating costs, as well as cost increases due to customer requests he never billed for. He had based his projected profits solely on costs associated with the sale of his services. Meanwhile, his overhead had crept upward unexpectedly—higher rents, a spike in energy costs, a cluster of critical equipment repairs. Worse, after he had signed a contract with his biggest client, one of his major suppliers folded, forcing him into emergency negotiations with a vendor who knew he had Don over a barrel and stuck him with a higher price.

Don's predicament is more common than you might think. You can have all the sales you want, but if you don't aggressively manage your costs, you can quickly sink. And it can be worse if you don't know where you really stand in the profit game.

Sometimes the profit margins get squeezed because the business owner doesn't have a clear idea of what "making a profit" actually means. Let me ask you a question: Would you rather own a business with $10 million in sales and $100,000 in profit, or one with $1 million in sales and $300,000 in profits? You'd be surprised at how many business people choose the former. They measure business success by total sales revenue or the number of people they employ.

They're wrong, of course. If you're spending every cent

you take in, what's the difference whether your total annual sales are $1,000 or $1 billion? All that matters in the end is the bottom line, what you earn. To put it another way, it's not what you sell, it's what you keep: *profit.*

The common measure used to gauge profit is *profit margin,* the percentage of your total sales that becomes profit. In its simplest terms, profit margin is profit divided by revenue (or sales):

Your revenue	$10.00
Your total cost	− $8.10
Net profit	$1.90
Profit margin	$1.90 ÷ $10.00 = 0.19 = 19%

You should calculate your profit margin on several levels of your business: when analyzing an individual project, evaluating a collection of sales, or reviewing your total annual sales. Be sure to include every revenue and cost line item, anything that's directly associated with the delivery of your services or goods–manufacturing and product costs, sales expenses, commissions, delivery, etc. Also include a proportional allocation of fixed overhead expenses that you pay to keep the doors of your business open: rent, clerical staff, copy machine, taxes, etc. Factor in projected increases in all expenses, and just to be safe, pad your costs by adding a couple of percentage points. You can "line item" this as contingency or hedge costs.

Projecting profit margins helps you make informed decisions about future sales efforts. Say you produce two products, on one of which you project a margin of 17 percent, the other 13 percent (margins vary widely between industries). All else being equal, the former is your better option. Without looking at the potential profit margin for each product, you might not know which way to go. This is especially important when projecting large sales to your biggest customers.

> **All that matters in the end is the bottom line. It's not what you sell, it's what you keep: profit.**

The loss of a tiny percent in your profit margin can become a huge problem when you're committed to a high-dollar, long-term contract. Your Elephant might use its considerable power to hold you to your commitment. It might also, if you let it, squeeze you so hard that you end up actually losing money—which, as you are probably aware, is not the best way to run a business.

Let's say you've signed the papers with the Elephant of your dreams and are excited about all the money you're going to make. Everything goes along smoothly for a few months; then your Elephant starts asking for more services—more reports, more customer service, higher-quality components, rush deliveries, more in-person meetings requiring costly travel.

You think, We'd better keep this Elephant happy, and you begin providing the extras at no additional cost. But if you don't understand the impact these extras have on your profit margin, you may be giving away the store. Maybe you think it's petty to charge for these extras, that the Elephant will lose respect for you if you even mention it. That's unlikely. Look at it this way: would the Elephant encourage its own financial officers to give away products or services?

If you decide not to charge for the extras, at least you'll have done your analysis, and you'll know exactly the impact it will have on your profits.

Like you, an Elephant is in business to make a profit. It will explore every nook and cranny looking for ways to save pennies, which, in a large business, can quickly add up to enormous sums. The Elephant might look to squeeze a few of those pennies out of you. If the Elephant feels that you're an easy mark or that added services really don't cost you anything because you've not charged for them, it might squeeze a little harder, and then a little harder.

Don't let it get to the point where you have to complain. When the Elephant asks for extras, simply provide a quote and remember to bill for them. Rather than alienating your customer, you will probably gain its respect as an experienced business operation, one that watches its pennies as diligently as the Elephant itself. Besides, what good is the client's goodwill when your entire business goes the way of the passenger pigeon? Of what use is the Elephant's happiness to your unpaid suppliers? Your creditors? Your investors? If you decide in the end not to charge for the extras, at least you'll have done your analysis, and you'll know exactly the impact it will have on your profits, which is the real point of monitoring your margins.

Of course, you should never blindside your big customer; a surprised Elephant is a dangerous animal. Part of your normal business operation should be simple, regular reports to the client. When you provide a value or respond to a request that is not understood to be part of your contract, report it promptly, show what it costs, and indicate the extra charge on your invoice. The Elephant can then decide whether it wants to continue receiving the extras under those conditions or, perhaps, negotiate with you for a better deal. If you lose the extras, you lose both the income and the expense—but you won't take a hit to your margin, and you won't lose the Elephant's respect.

Respect should work both ways. If you've negotiated a deal that's good for both you and your client, then get hit out of the blue with a sudden, unforeseeable, catastrophic rise in costs, you should try to renegotiate your deal. It's not beyond the realm of possibility for a hurricane to wipe out half of your production capacity or for an action by an overseas government to double the price of an essential component. The blow could put you out of business, and if that happened, your Elephant might suffer, too.

Suppose an international political event caused your energy costs to rise 30 percent overnight. What's your Elephant's best interest? To let you sink while it goes out and finds another supplier? Chances are the next vendor would have the same energy costs, and the Elephant would end up paying as much or more than if it had negotiated a new deal with you, its longtime and experienced friend. Always keep renegotiation in mind as a possible way out of difficulty. It can't hurt to ask.

> When you provide a value that is not in your contract, report it promptly, show what it costs, and indicate the extra charge on your invoice.

Once you get comfortable with the idea of providing extra services—and charging for them—you'll find that fulfilling such requests can actually increase your profit margin. Respond to them positively. Most Elephants will not object to paying for them.

Plan, Monitor, and Evaluate

Depending on your business and industry, you should be able to develop a budget for every project, contract, or billing cycle. This planned or projected budget becomes operational when you and your client agree on a price.

A budget doesn't need to be complex, sophisticated, or expensive. I use a template created for me by a small CPA firm, a simple Excel spreadsheet, to print out periodic budget reports. All I have to do is plug in revenue and cost figures, and the results are calculated automatically. It cost me less than $500.

You can do the same, no matter what your business. Basically, the report should have three columns: budgeted numbers, actual numbers, and variance from budget. On the cost side, include all incremental activities you are doing for your Elephant, along with their dollar costs to you; on the revenue side, show what you've billed the Elephant for these activities.

You should run this report often, at least once a month. This lets you monitor project costs as you proceed and, if necessary, make adjustments to maintain your margin. When the project is complete, run a final check to see how your actual profit compares with your initial budget projections. You and your team can then evaluate each budget line item and decide how to change your operations to keep your margins where you want them.

Your business may have its own accounting staff to help with these and many other kinds of business analysis. If so, have your accountants create the kind of system we're talking about here. It's simple.

I know most of you would prefer to work on improving your product or service or on marketing it, but it's that third leg of the three-legged stool—managing your budget—that can make the real difference in your profits. If your business is still small or you wish to outsource these services, find a small CPA firm; it will be well worth the cost.

Project Your Cash Flow

Monitoring is one thing; projecting is another. You can start driving your car from here to Walla Walla, but if you keep your eyes locked on your dashboard gauges, you'll probably end up in the ditch. In a project, you should be monitoring your business to keep track of where you are, how you're doing, and whether you have enough cash to operate at any given instant–but you also need to be looking down the road to see where you'll be in one month, six months, or a year. If it's not somewhere you want to be, now's the time to take corrective action.

Cash flow projections are your way of looking down the road. Use a simple spreadsheet program or ask your financial people or accounting firm to project your cash flow a reasonable interval into the future. If you can see that you're going to be temporarily short of cash in October and November, unable to pay your employees or your vendors, you can do something about it in advance.

Here are actions every business should take in order to manage its cash flow:

Know your current payables and receivables. I'm amazed at how many business and professional people are unaware of these two basic concepts. Run a weekly report outlining your current cash position, accounts receivable, and accounts payable. Make sure it includes any big charges you might be expecting.

If necessary, negotiate with suppliers. Build a delayed-payment time frame into your agreement with suppliers in case you get paid late by your Elephant. Since you probably don't have Elephant buying power, you'll have to negotiate this up front. It may cost you a supplier or two who won't be willing to delay their billing, but there will be several who will, especially in return for more business. This way, you're partners, and as the Elephant helps you, it also helps your supplier.

Draw up a bank contingency plan. If you haven't done so already, start developing a solid relationship with a financial institution such as a bank—the sooner the better.

Who Says All Lawyers Are Bad?

I've been actively involved in a healthcare business based in London. We're a startup, having only been going at it for about two years. The business latched on to a pretty big idea, which resulted in obtaining government healthcare contracts valued at a staggering $500 million! Our Elephant was the National Healthcare System of England.

The company started out with a much smaller vision but through luck, flexibility, and tenacity quickly reshaped itself into a different business to capitalize on this huge opportunity.

The problem was that the business was funded to grow steadily, but this new opportunity required a lot more money. We couldn't just sit on the sidelines until we raised some money, so we went to some of our key suppliers to see what we could do to shake loose some cash.

We went first to our biggest supplier—our attorneys, a prominent firm with offices around the world. They had done quite a bit of work for us, reviewing detailed government bids, writing and reviewing contracts, and consulting on new business development. We'd paid them a significant amount already and knew we were only scratching the surface of what we'd actually be needing.

They didn't give us any cash, but after some tapdancing, this firm agreed to defer their invoices for almost six months. They said they believed in our company, its management, and, most of all, the marketplace.

They also knew they stood a great chance of getting all of our legal work, and although the risk of our insolvency was certainly there, the potential for a huge windfall was too big to ignore.

As business went ahead, things did get a bit tense. The company missed the first payment-due date. The lawyers were obviously concerned, but because we kept them informed about our business and its successes, they felt reassured that it was only a matter of time before they were paid. Another six months went by and fees mounted to over $1 million. They continued to work.

Their patience and forbearance allowed us to survive in a cash-drained environment, but it paid off for them as well. Several months later, when our funding finally came in, we had missed their targeted year-end due date. This put them in a bit of a spot with their corporate office, but concerns evaporated when we immediately paid them $1.5 million in fees off the top. We had become their biggest client in the United Kingdom—their Elephant.

One way to establish goodwill and a credit history is to borrow money, even if you don't need to, and pay it back on time. If you already have a business loan outstanding, good. Make sure to spend a little time on that relationship as well. Then, when your cash flow projections show lean times six months ahead, you can let your banker know the situation in advance and arrange to have funds available to keep your business going until you're back in the black.

Most business owners and professionals avoid bankers like the plague, feeling that if they're too visible they might get their notes called in. The truth is that banks appreciate being kept informed of your financial progress. Share your vision, projections, even your business plan. Make them see just how great your business is and how close you are to success with your Elephants; this will help you when your note comes up for review, or in case you need to borrow short-term against your receivables. It's not a bad idea to include your banker in your customer mailings or other marketing efforts. And remember that once your Elephant pays out and you're flush with cash, you'll be a valued customer at the bank, so don't feel bad asking them to support you for a while.

Create your own investor network. Make a list of people who might like to invest in your business—family members as well as outside investors. Keep them informed on how well your business is doing, especially your progress with big customers. Their desire to lend you money will depend largely on their comfort level and knowledge of your business. That's why this preparatory work is vital if you need to call on them in time of crisis. Remember, Noah built the ark before the rain!

Even when I had a small business with only four employees, I always turned out a short company newsletter every month. This would include positive news on the business, including potential new customers, employee accomplishments, maybe even a recent case study or two. I made sure to include the bank and my investor network in the mailings. This usually did the trick.

Finally, if you're still haunted by the occasional vision of yourself standing on the corner with a squeegee and a tin cup, keep a current business plan handy for quick update and dissemination should you need to raise funds quickly.

Is There an Elephant in Your Future?

Well, you've stayed with me all the way to the end of this book. For that, I'd like to thank you, because it means I've engaged your business smarts and imagination in some of the ways I wanted to. It also means that you feel the journey has been interesting and worthwhile. Either that or your alternative was a six-hour car ride with the in-laws.

Now that we're finished with the part where I write and you read, I want to encourage you once again to take me up on my offer of free information and tools to help you bag your Elephant. I invite you to go to my Web site, **www.stevekaplanlive.com**, and click on "Pachyderm Café" in the top navigation bar, then "Free Stuff." This site is both a free resource and a gateway into other products and services designed to help you and your business succeed. The free resources include templates, tactical materials, and more. I put the tools here as a supplement to the book to help you put the Bag the Elephant concepts into action. If you're interested in additional resources, you can find these on the site as well, but regardless, you should check out the free stuff.

At this point, however, I symbolically step down from the podium and move to the back of the auditorium, where I will turn over the Elephant bagging to you.

As I depart, I'd like to leave you with two bits of advice.

Bit of advice #1: Be the Elephant. If you get nothing else from this book, try to put yourself inside the mind of the Elephant. Think of it as acting or role-playing: You are the Elephant. As a (suddenly) giant corporation, what is important to you? What do you expect from your vendors, from your suppliers, and from the owners of smaller businesses, sales reps, and professionals with private practices who want to offer their services and products to you? How would you like and expect to be treated? When you're thinking about buying, what features, what practices, what attitudes make you look more favorably on the seller?

Bit of advice #2: Befriend your Elephant. One of the greatest advantages of the Elephant strategy is that it compels you to form a close relationship with your Elephant, for that is the true path to long-term riches. If you're not using the Elephant strategy, you have to have many, many customers paying small amounts. You can, and you should, maintain relationships with them—but because there are so many of them, these relationships cannot be as deep. With the Bag the Elephant strategy, you embed yourself and your company so deeply into the fabric of the Elephant that you become like gum in the carpet—you're there for the duration.

Learn to think like the Elephant; develop deep and meaningful relationships based on mutual trust, respect, and success. Think of it as maximizing your return on your Elephant investment.

Thank you for your time and energy. Now put down the book and go Bag Your Elephant!

Afterword: Beyond *Bag the Elephant!*

One of the best things about putting out a new edition of a bestseller like *Bag the Elephant!* is that I can talk about things that I know will make the book even more useful. I can do that because lots of people have read the book and written to tell me about how it helped them, or to offer new insights into the subject matter, or to ask questions that they couldn't find answers for in the book. In other words, I can talk about stuff I—oops!—forgot to include the first time around.

Since writing *Bag the Elephant!*, I've delivered hundreds of speeches and communicated with thousands of business owners and sales professionals in many countries. Using the book as a guide, many of them have bagged one or more Elephants or signed bigger contracts with their current big clients. One business owner wrote that she wrangled a deal to supply specialty parts to a large appliance company, boosting the number of sales from 2,500 per year to 3,000 per month and annual revenues from $185,000 to $2.2 million over two years. (Having learned from the book, she prepared for the sales surge before the contract was signed by going to her banker to arrange a loan to expand plant capacity.)

And then there was the sales manager for a mid-size tire wholesaler who followed a personal connection to a champion within a large auto-dealers' association; he quadrupled his sales force's contracts within twelve months.

Great successes. But regardless of the size of their business, many business people wanted to know what was needed to get to the next level—namely, how to assess and motivate their sales professionals to concentrate on their Elephant hunting. For them, bagging the Elephant is still the number-one factor in their success or the number-one obstacle to achieving it.

Here are a few of the questions they've been asking me.

Light a Fire

"We talk a lot in my company about getting the big customer, but talk is cheap and results are not up to expectations. I'm committed to Elephant bagging as the mainstay of my sales strategy. How can I motivate my sales force to join me and go after those big customers?"

John G., Boston technology firm

Everyone knows that owners have to support their sales force's efforts, yet many salespeople feel that management is locking horns with them. Here are some ways you can keep your sales force motivated and effective:

Must Haves

Salespeople believe they need several kinds of support from the company in order to achieve success:

Solid execution. Salespeople want the items they sell to be delivered correctly and on time. If they're selling direct through retail, they expect all items to be in stock, unless they've been notified otherwise.

Timely quotes. They need to know what to charge, without unnecessary delays that could kill the momentum of the sale.

Timely payments. Salespeople expect to be paid their commissions and bonuses in a fair and timely manner.

Sales materials. They must have materials that they feel will enhance their ability to sell.

Consistency. Businesses that too often change pay scales, accounts, or territories fill a sales force with uncertainty.

Bonuses. Salespeople expect some consideration if they pull out all stops to meet a bonus target but miss it by a hair. If you treat the near-winners the same as those who don't even come close, you'll build resentment. Find some sort of middle ground for these folks.

Nice to Have

These tactics won't necessarily cause motivation to skyrocket in the short term, but they can do wonders for long-term performance:

Status. Many salespeople relish the chance to have the company president or senior management come along on a sales call. It confirms their status to the client and makes them feel good about their standing in the company. The same goes for helping in-house staff on sales presentations and pitches.

Professionalism. A well-run sales meeting can improve morale. It should be businesslike but convivial, at times even with good food and drink, as well as well-timed breaks.

Contests. An in-house competition can give you a quick sales bump. Develop contests that let you recognize all employees who participate in the sales process—administrative staff, account managers, and others. Base awards not only on sales figures and the biggest increase over last year, but also on more subjective criteria, the most important new sale, the sale with the biggest potential for repeat, even the best proposal that didn't result in a sale. Be creative; develop awards that uniquely fit your business. To keep things light, I often include amusing categories, such as funniest sales call. This gives salespeople a chance to bond by sharing their horror stories: forgetting to bring sales materials, cooling their heels when buyers didn't show up, cutting loose with a garlicky belch in an after-lunch sales meeting.

Creature comforts. If your staff is working late, spring for a pizza. Your twenty-dollar investment will pay dividends.

Above and Beyond

Surprising sales staff with unexpected benefits can spell the difference between pretty good performance and outstanding results:

Perks. Going the extra mile deepens staff loyalty and makes them feel that your business is the best place to work.

Parties or entertainment. Sociable by nature, salespeople get a kick out of holiday parties, employee picnics, Broadway shows, and the like—the more creative the better. It's the "work hard, play hard" mentality that you're looking for.

Time off. Surprise hardworking salespeople with a day off. It will rejuvenate them and soften the blow of the next late-night project.

Special bonuses. Holiday bonuses or annual bonuses go a long way. But if you dole them out every year regardless of performance, they'll be taken for granted.

Set Fair Compensation

"What's the best commission structure for motivating my sales force? I want to make sure that they have the incentive to earn huge commissions by selling a ton of services."

Michele C., Atlanta marketing company

Total pay includes commissions, salaries, bonuses, and benefits. Because salespeople see their pay as a reflection of themselves, compensation can be your greatest management tool. To be fair to yourself and your salespeople, you need to link compensation to profitability.

Overall pay level. Remember to include the value of your entire compensation package, including benefits, when setting your policy.

Bonuses. If you pay bonuses, tie them to company profitability as well as to individual accomplishment. Linking bonuses with companywide results helps you avoid overpaying one or two salespeople when your business has a particularly bad year.

Targets. Make sure your salespeople understand how meeting goals and objectives will affect their total pay package.

Commissions

Commissions are the most important part of any good salesperson's pay package—but setting up commission structures is also where business owners make the most common mistakes. Take the following example:

Your charge to the customer	$14.00
Your cost for your product or service	$10.00
Gross company profit	$4.00 (28% profit margin: $4÷$14)

But what if your salesperson receives a 5 percent commission on every sale? For a more realistic profit projection, deduct commissions from your gross profits. Now look at the numbers:

Your charge to the customer	$14.00
Cost for your product or service	$10.00
Profit before commission	$4.00
5% commission on $14	$0.70
Net company profit	$3.30 (23.5% profit margin: $3.30÷$14)

Now let's say your salesperson had to reduce the price to $12.50 because of competition or other reasons:

Your charge to the customer	$12.50
Cost of your product or service	$10.00
Profit before commission	$2.50
5% commission on $12.50	$0.63
Net company profit	$1.87 (15% profit margin: $1.87÷$12.50)

In each of these situations your salesperson is getting a full 5 percent commission on the sale price, while your profit margin is shrinking.

You can avoid this common trap by treating your salespeople as partners. Like you, they should have a stake in the prices the company charges. If they sell at the projected price, great. If not, their commission should be reduced commensurately.

I abide by this principle with a firm commission structure that accounts for salespeople selling at slightly reduced pricing. Here's an example:

Sell Price	Commission
Full price	5.0%
Up to 10% off	4.5%
10.1%–15% off	3.75%
15.1%–20% off	2.0%

Sales Targets

When setting sales targets, resist pressure from your salespeople to lower quotas, even though they will offer no end of reasons to do so. Set goals that are attainable but that still make them stretch. To establish quotas for salespeople who have been around a while, use their historical sales data as a starting point, then tack on another 10 percent. I always assume that my salespeople will attain, on average, 75 percent of their collective target, so I adjust each quota accordingly to ensure adequate aggregate sales. I also use about 75 percent of the targeted sales quotas on financial statements projecting revenues for the upcoming year.

Analyze Sales Performance

"How do I know who my best salespeople are? Is it based solely on who sells the most?"

Sandy J., Dallas specialty foods company

I've developed a useful way to gauge the effectiveness of a sales staff. I call it the **value quotient**. It has two components: **a sales value quotient** and a **profit value quotient.** In some cases, you'll learn—as I have—that salespeople you thought were top performers have actually been costing you nearly as much as they've been earning for you. The value quotient helps you determine whether that's the case, and it gives you the ammunition you need to take the necessary action.

Perform the following calculations for each salesperson (if you don't know the numbers for each step, take that as a huge red flag; the first thing you should do is take the time to figure them out):

1. Start with the salesperson's total sales for the year (use her projections if the year isn't over).
2. List the company's average profit margin from her sales, before commissions (profit margin is the company profit from a sale divided by the customer's cost on that sale). This number indicates how much your company is making on that salesperson's sales, expressed as a percent of the sale price.
3. Determine the cost of the salesperson's total annual compensation (salary, commissions, bonuses, employment taxes, and benefits).

4. Divide the salesperson's total costs to you by her total annual sales. The result is the SALES VALUE QUOTIENT. The lower the number, the better for your bottom line.

5. Divide the salesperson's total costs to you by the profit she brings in each year. The result is the PROFIT VALUE QUOTIENT. Here, too, the lower the better.

6. The profit value quotient is where the rubber meets the road. Have you ever wondered: of the profits a salesperson brings into the company, what percentage goes to her rather than to the company? The profit value quotient is that figure.

Here's an example for three salespeople.

	Joe Smith	Deborah Hayes	Bill Jones
Sales	$195,000	$300,000	$600,000
Average Profit Margin	35%	25%	20%
Profit	**66,500**	**75,000**	**120,000**
Salary	15,000	20,000	50,000
Commissions	5,000	8,000	30,000
Benefits	1,200	1,200	1,500
Bonus	0	1,000	2,000
Taxes	9,000	14,400	28,000
Total Cost of Salesperson	**30,200**	**45,200**	**115,500**
Sales Value Quotient	.15 or 15%	.15 or 15%	.19 or 19%
Profit Value Quotient	.45 or 45%	.60 or 60%	.96 or 96%

These examples show that although Bill is selling more than Joe or Deborah, his net effect on the company isn't as favorable as you might think. It turns out that both Joe and Deborah are doing more good for the business because their profit value quotients are much lower. In fact, Bill's profit value quotient of .96 means that 96 percent of the profit he earns for the company ends up in his pocket. That's right—for every dollar profit, Bill gets 96 cents and your company gets 4 cents.

Further analysis of the numbers shows why: although Bill is paid more than the other two, the real killer is that he sells at lower margins (20 percent)—that's probably how he meets his sales quotas and gets his bonuses—but still receives the same 5 percent commission on sales. It's time to have a talk with Bill and come up with a new plan that's fair to all parties.

Get Ready to Rumble

"My business is slowly failing. As time goes on, revenues have remained stagnant while costs have continued to rise. Now I think I've finally cracked that big customer. I desperately need the new business, but I'm concerned that I won't be able to execute on the contract. Any ideas?"

Maria F., Los Angeles franchise owner

Believe it or not, fear of success is more common than you might think, and many people are not used to dealing with success at this level. But believe me when I tell you this: with proper planning and the core values outlined in this book, you'll be all set.

If you're truly the kind of person who fears success, perhaps business isn't for you. You're either on the Elephant track or you're not. If you're on board, then follow the path and go all out. Draw up your Mock Elephant Plan, as described in "Operational Explosion" (chapter 17), to make sure you're set to handle the growth. Then execute the plan, Bag the Elephant, and have a bunch of fun!

And here's my sales plug: For more information on how to set up processes to handle your organizational and customer growth in your company, plus other strategies to grow your business, pick up a copy of my other book: *Be the Elephant: Build a Bigger BETTER Business.*

A Plan for All Seasons

"Using Bag the Elephant! *as a guide, I turned my small business into a large, thriving concern. Now I wonder, Is the Bag the Elephant philosophy applicable only to business, or can I use it to achieve other things?"*

Jack T., Cleveland sales trainer

I love this question, because bagging the Elephant is not just a business strategy, it's a whole mindset—a way of thinking, an approach to life that can bring you success in any endeavor. I use it in every aspect of my life. It has become automatic; I do it without thinking.

In the books I've written, the Elephant represents a big company. But really, the Elephant is a symbol that can stand for whatever you want. Suppose, for example, you want to meet and spend some time with that great gal or guy you see at Starbucks. There are three approaches you can take:

- Do nothing (which is what most people do).
- Walk up, engage in witty banter, and ask for a date (in other words, cold call and prepare to be rejected).
- Draw up a plan to Bag the Elephant. (It helps if you avoid thinking of an Elephant solely in terms of size.)

Bagging the Elephant can involve several key tactics:

- Talk with your friends to find out who knows your intended and who has dating influence (chapter 4: "What to Know About Elephants").
- Once you learn who knows her, try to turn a mutual friend into your champion (chapter 11: "Recruiting Great Champions").
- Do further reconnaissance on what types of music, food, sport, or hobbies interest the person (chapter 4: "What to Know About Elephants").

- Now you're ready to call. Don't leave a message; present yourself in person (chapter 7: "Knocking on Doors").

Now, there's much more to it than this, of course. I didn't sign on to be your dating guru, and the results you achieve may vary (I can't be responsible for your personal choices). But with a little reflection, you'll see that the Bag the Elephant philosophy can be a great way to pursue your dreams and aspirations, whatever they are and whatever their size and audacity.

Just be sure it's the Elephant you want.

—*Steve Kaplan*

Acknowledgments

I'd like to thank the following people, without whose help and support the book wouldn't have been possible:

Thanks to my first and favorite Elephant, the wonderful professionals and visionary innovators at Procter & Gamble: Lori Crowe, Jackie Cunningham, Rad Ewing, Glenna Galbrieth, Mindy Patton, Jerry Preece, Margo Ross, Randy Sadler, Brett Stover, Cindy Tripp, Karen Ventura, Pat Volmering, Deb Walker, and many, many others.

Thanks to the greatest Elephant-bagging team ever assembled: Duane Clement, Holly Graham, Chris Joy, Denise Kaplan, Steve Ludkowski, Kristin Mattimore, Sherry Orel, Jesse Reif, Steve Rogin, Tara Steele, and Marty Struck. I'll never forget all the great times we had!

Thanks to those of you who were nice enough to take time out of your busy lives to read portions of the manuscript and provide invaluable feedback: Duane Clement, Tom Connellan, Molly Gordon, Brendi Kaplan, Denise Kaplan, Ella Moore, Paul Weinberg, and Robert D. Workman.

Thanks to David Hahn and the folks at Planned Television Arts for their comprehensive and innovative publicity campaign: Jared Sharpe, Minsun Pak, Virginia Quiambao, and Dennelle Catlett.

Thank you to Peter Workman and everyone at Team Workman.

Thanks to J. J. for your creative inspiration.

Thanks, Mike Drew, for your never-ending tenacity and marketing savvy that went far beyond what was expected. Your total commitment and focus on every single detail of the process was uncanny. Everyone should use you as a required team member when publishing a book.

Thank you, Jeff Morris, for your technical expertise, your creative flair, and your 25-hour-a-day effort in editing, designing, and generating the pulse of the book. I couldn't even think of writing another book without you.

Thank you, Ray Bard, for your leadership, innovation, and brilliance. I really enjoyed learning from such a pro.

About the Author

Steve Kaplan, author of the *New York Times* bestseller *Be the Elephant,* has made a career of shepherding businesses to success and helping others do the same. Turning Sampling Corporation of America (SCA), a basement operation, into a $250 million, 1,300-employee marketing company spanning sixteen countries was only the beginning. Over the past twenty years, he has helped more than one hundred businesses of all sizes and industries get big customers, restructure themselves, improve efficiency, boost morale, expand into new markets, and evaluate exit strategies, among other things. Recently he has been the managing partner in a venture specializing in providing equity and operating strategy to a range of businesses.

As an expert entrepreneur, Steve has been recognized by *Inc.* magazine as a finalist for Entrepreneur of the Year and has won the Mercury Excellence Award in Employee Motivation. He has been the subject of many print interviews and profiles at home and abroad in such media as *Advertising Age, Crain's Business, Food & Beverage, Selling, Target Marketing,* and the *Chicago Tribune.* His business practices have been featured in several college textbooks.

A graduate of Bradley University in Peoria, Illinois, Steve received his MBA from Rosary Graduate School of Business in River Grove, Illinois. He has taught courses in advertising, marketing, and business organization at Triton College in River Grove, Illinois. He is a sought-after public speaker, presenting keynote speeches and workshops for businesses of all sizes on many business topics. He has appeared on a variety of media (including CBS, NBC, and Fox Television) to discuss his experiences and insights. He has also written articles for business magazines such as *Target Marketing*. He is a *New York Times, Wall Street Journal, Business Week,* and *USA Today* bestselling author.

Steve's vision and leadership made BountySCA Worldwide one of the world's leading marketing service, database, and media organizations. He was a member of the executive committee of EuroRSCG, a 176-company conglomerate, and is the founder of The Difference Maker Inc., a company providing packaged tools and advice across a variety of business disciplines. He is also the owner of the investment firm Kaplan Enterprises LLC and a partner in eSkape, a 60,000-square-foot Chicago-area family entertainment center.

Steve chairs the Kaplan Family Foundation, a private foundation dedicated to the advancement of entrepreneurship in the youth of today.

Steve believes that both business *and* life should be an adventure and that both should be pursued with passion and vigor. Some of the adventures Steve has been fortunate to experience include: scuba diving with hammerhead sharks in the Galapagos Islands and whale sharks in the Chale Islands, Africa; running with the bulls in Pamplona, Spain; ski paragliding in Verbier, France; bungee jumping; gorilla trekking in the Congo; whitewater rafting; hot air ballooning over the Masa Mara, Africa; and body rafting in New Zealand.

About Nellie

Nellie is a twenty-one-year-old African elephant whose many skills include painting, basketball, baseball, swimming, music (harmonica), dancing, and spraying water. A talented bilingual (English and Swahili) actor, Nellie has made hundreds of appearances in person, on screens big and small, in everything from *Jackass* to *Money* magazine. She also lends her considerable presence (8,500 pounds, ten feet tall) and talents to numerous educational and charitable causes. She is trained by educational instructor Brian McMillan and represented by agent Vikki McMillan. She lives in the Los Angeles area.

The Difference
Maker Inc.

W hat is The Difference Maker Inc.? It's something I wish I had had when I was building my businesses. When I was starting out, I had no time to join "presidents groups." And since I was the one in charge, I had no one to kick around ideas with. Family and friends, however supportive, lacked the knowledge and experience to provide any meaningful advice. Books targeting businesses didn't really focus on the key issues that confronted me. I hungered for guidance from people I could trust, advice about proven strategies and tactics that I could implement to make an immediate difference in my business. But no one ever took a stance and said "Do this" or "Do that." I had to learn on my own, by trial and error.

That's why I created The Difference Maker Inc., a business that fills that void for those who wish to pursue success by following in my footsteps. It does so by providing the advice, leadership, and practical know-how that I couldn't find. (Go to **www.stevekaplanlive.com.**)

I've structured the service lines of The Difference Maker Inc. around the factors that have the greatest impact on business success. If you can succeed in these facets of business, you're well on your way to big-time success!

Rock Solid! Your Business on Solid Footing. This category of service focuses on the areas critical to success from the planning and business architecture perspective, with the objective of generating the best business model possible. Issues featured include: (1) business models, (2) projections, (3) generating assumptions, (4) using projections to shape your business, (5) assessing risks, (6) statements you really need, and (7) business viability and assessment.

Bag the Elephant: Getting Big Customers. This service line focuses on how to get the big customer, the one that can change your life. It includes: (1) positioning your business for the Elephant, (2) five things to know about big companies, (3) embracing bureaucracy, (4) finding your ideal prospects, (5) knocking on doors, (6) meeting your prospects, (7) picking champions, (8) building alliances, and (9) deadly perils to avoid in Elephant Land.

Be the Elephant: Growth and Value Strategies. This service line details my method for expanding a business and maximizing its value. Included are: (1) my ten steps to business expansion, (2) white space analysis, (3) growth strategy options, (4) assessing viability, (5) operations outlook, (6) why customers really buy, (7) creating value, (8) USPs and more.

Squeeze the Tube: Getting the Most from Your Employees. Business owners typically credit much of their success—or failure—to their employees. I've found that the biggest concern for business owners is how to identify and retain good employees and maximize their potential. This service line focuses on: (1) the three indispensable human elements I've most often encountered, (2) eight principles of leadership, (3) motivation, (4) the pyramid of salespeople's needs, (5) managing your salespeople, (6) value sales quotient, and (7) performers versus nonperformers.

Just Desserts! Selling Your Business. This service line tells exactly what is needed to get your business and yourself ready for a potential sale, what to expect during the sale, and how to prepare for life thereafter. Included are: (1) understanding and mastering deal structures, (2) the closing process, (3) developing a platform for negotiations, (4) hiring the right representative to get the most from your sales, and (5) demonstrating the due diligence purchasers are looking for.

At **www.stevekaplanlive.com,** you can learn more about the service lines, as well as these other products and services:

Business Boost **free e-newsletter.**

This is a high-quality, thought-provoking source for actionable tips, advice, and real-world success stories straight from the trenches, in all disciplines. You'll get big-customer tactics from the Bag the Elephant line, strategies to grow your business from the Be the Elephant line, plus some of the best resources around. This newsletter will help you define yourself as a leader, shape your business for success, even increase the sale value of your business—and it's free!

The Difference Maker Workshops.

These are intensive three-day programs focusing on issues most critical to the business. Each workshop includes material from each service line, with break-out sessions to address and analyze attendees' specific issues.

Toolboxes with Power Tools.

This is a partner and resource I really wish I had had: fifteen years of experience rolled into simple, effective, step-by-step strategies and tactics to help your business succeed, available at the click of a mouse. The Power Tools are proprietary detailed charts, templates, and worksheets that facilitate your use of the toolbox material in your own business.

Steve—One-on-One.

This individual program is tailored to meet the specific needs of your business. Whether it's working with your management on organizational issues, training your team to get that BIG customer, developing successful growth strategies to expand your business, or that keynote address at your annual meeting, these sessions will have a major impact.

Index